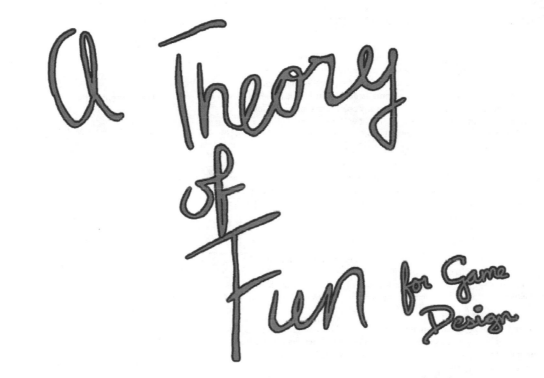

A Theory of Fun for Game Design

BY RAPH KOSTER

PARAGLYPH
PRESS

A Theory of Fun for Game Design

Paraglyph Press, Inc.
4015 N. 78th Street, #115
Scottsdale, Arizona 85251
Phone: 602-749-8787
www.paraglyphpress.com

Paraglyph Press ISBN: 1-932111-97-2

Printed in the United States of America
16 15 14 13 12   [2012-09-14]

PRESIDENT
Keith Weiskamp

EDITOR-AT-LARGE
Jeff Duntemann

VICE PRESIDENT, SALES, MARKETING, AND DISTRIBUTION
Steve Sayre

VICE PRESIDENT, INTERNATIONAL SALES AND MARKETING
Cynthia Caldwell

PRODUCTION MANAGER
Kim Eoff

DEVELOPMENT EDITOR
Ben Sawyer

COVER ARTIST
Raph Koster

COVER DESIGNER
Kris Sotelo

WHAT PEOPLE ARE SAYING!

"*A Theory of Fun* elucidates some basic truths that apply not just to games but to all entertainment. Even better, it does so in a style that is clear, insightful, and... fun! I expect this book to become an instant classic, fascinating to anyone who has ever made a game—or played one."
— Noah Falstein, Freelance Game Designer/Writer/Producer

"A book about fun which is actually fun to read. It reminds me of Scott McCloud's *Understanding Comics*—a work which makes sophisticated arguments by pulling them down to basic principles and presenting them in an engaging fashion. Raph Koster offers a road map for how to make games an even more expressive medium."
— Henry Jenkins, Director, MIT's Comparative Media Studies Program.

"Raph has been an inspiration to countless developers over the years. His focus on finding new ways to communicate complex design issues has been an incredible benefit to the international game developers, who crowd into his lectures. Finally, he's tackling probably the most important principle of all, the one that all game designers someday need to become the masters of... "Making things Fun!""
— David Perry, President Shiny Entertainment (Atari, Inc.)

"Does for games what *Understanding Comics* did for sequential art. Non-gamers: Buy this for the gamer in your life. Gamers: Buy this for the non-gamer in your life. You'll never look at fun the same way again."
— Cory Doctorow, Author of *Eastern Standard Tribe* and *Down and Out in the Magic Kingdom*; co-editor of Boing Boing

"Gaming is much more than having fun—it is core to being human. Understanding games, and fun, helps us understand ourselves. Raph Koster is one of the good guys, always working to make more fun in our world. With this book he's just helped all of us, his readers and students, do exactly that."
— Mike McShaffry, Author of *Game Coding Complete* and Head of Studio at Breakaway Games

"Amazing! All-New! Only Available on TV! Koster's *A Theory of Fun* is well-written, timely, passionate and scientifically informed, a fine piece of work that's bound to get lots of well-deserved attention."
— Edward Castronova, Associate Professor of Telecommunications, Indiana University

"Raph Koster asks the important question about games: why are they fun, and what does that say about games and about us? Koster takes our love of games at face value—we play them because they are fun, we hate them when they are boring—and he assumes the art of game design is to get more of the former and less of the latter."
— Clay Shirky, Adjunct Professor, Interactive Telecommunications Program, NYU

Raph Koster was born in 1971, has lived in four countries and over a half-dozen different states, and is married with two kids. He holds a bachelor's degree from Washington College in English/creative writing and in Spanish and a master of fine arts degree in creative writing from the University of Alabama. While in college, he also spent some time studying most everything in the humanities, including music theory and composition and studio art.

He never studied programming, but that didn't stop him from playing a key role on *LegendMUD,* an award-winning mud themed on "history the way they thought it was," which is still running after ten years at **www.legendmud.org**. Professionally, Raph was creative lead and lead designer on *Ultima Online* and *Ultima Online: The Second Age* and the creative director on *Star Wars Galaxies.* Collectively, these massively multiplayer titles have served as the virtual home away from home for well over two million people since 1997 and have won numerous awards.

Raph writes regularly on the subjects of game design, online communities, and virtual lives, including such well-known articles as "The Laws of Online World Design," "A Story About a Tree," and "Declaring the Rights of Players." Many of these texts are featured regularly on university syllabi. He is also a frequent speaker and keynoter at conferences ranging from the Game Developers Conference to legal and social policy conferences at Swiss Re and New York Law School.

In his spare time, Raph is a singer-songwriter and has released one CD, *After the Flood,* available via **www.cafepress.com/raphkoster**. He is also an occasional writer of science fiction and fantasy and a past member of the famed Turkey City SF writing workshop.

Raph currently resides in San Diego, California, where he is the chief creative officer at Sony Online Entertainment, the makers of *EverQuest, Planetside,* and *EverQuest II.*

His website is **www.legendmud.org/raph/**. You can also visit the book's official website at **www.theoryoffun.com** for access to a blog about the book and merchandise based on the cartoons.

DEDICATION

This book is dedicated to my kids,
without whom I never would have written it,
and to Kristen, because I always promised my first book would be for her.
Without her, there'd be no book.

ACKNOWLEDGEMENTS

hey, who wrote on me?

Special thanks to all those who have helped me clarify the thoughts that went into this book over the last few years, through their writing and direct conversation and by challenging my assumptions. In no particular order:

Cory Ondrejka for passionately dreaming the dream; Ben Cousins for coining "ludeme" and pursuing empirical approaches; David Kennerly for loving the ludemes; Gordon Walton and Rich Vogel for mentoring, mentoring, mentoring—and letting go; J. C. Lawrence for creating the forum; Jesper Juul for questioning the premise; Jessica Mulligan for opening the art question; John Buehler for the emotion questions; John Donham for indulging and interest; Lee Sheldon for insisting on story; Nicole Lazzaro for introducing me to research on emotion; Noah Falstein for treading down a similar path—keep an eye out for his book; Richard Bartle for the playspace, and for advocating authorial intent; Richard Garriott for injecting ethics; Rod Humble for listening to very long rambles; Sasha Hart for the human condition questions; Timothy Burke and many other players for forcing me to consider the question; Will Wright for insight into formal game systems.

Extra special thanks to those who helped make the book in this form come together: Kurt Squire for introducing Ben to the original presentation, Ben Sawyer for editing, Dave Taylor and Patricia Pizer for fantastic volunteer editing jobs, Keith Weiskamp for publishing and line-by-line commentary, Chris Nakashima-Brown for legal help, Kim Eoff for laying out the book, and Judy Flynn for copyediting.

Above all, to Kristen, who helped scan the images, gave me the space in which to work, and read the drafts as they emerged. Without the time granted to me by her willingness to watch the kids, cook the food, and keep me working, this would never have come to be.

Finally, thank you to all those who in my life have allowed me to pursue this crazy career. And to my family, for fostering the sense of fun from an early age and buying all the darn games and computers for me.

CONTENTS

FOREWORD BY WILL WRIGHT

The title of this book almost feels wrong to me. As a game designer, seeing the words "Theory" and "Fun" in such close proximity instinctively makes me a bit uncomfortable. Theories are dry and academic things, found in thick books at the back of the library, whereas fun is light, energetic, playful and…well…fun.

For the first few decades of interactive game design we were able to blithely ignore many of the larger meta-questions surrounding our craft while we slowly, painfully learned to walk. Now for the first time we are starting to see serious interest in what we do from the academic side. This is forcing those of us in the games industry to stop and consider,

"What is this new medium that we're working in?"

The academic interest seems twofold: First is the recognition that video games probably represent an emerging new medium, a new design field, and possibly a new art form. All of these are worthy of study. Second, there are an increasing number of motivated students that grew up playing these games and now find themselves inspired to work in the field one day. They want to find schools that will help them understand what games are and how to make them.

One slight problem: there are very few teachers that understand games well enough to teach them, no matter how motivated their students happen to be. Actually it's worse than that because there are very few people working in the games industry today (and Raph Koster is definitely one of them) who understand games well enough to even communicate what they know and how they know it.

The bridges between the game industry and the academics that want to study and teach games are slowly beginning to form. A shared language is developing, allowing both sides to speak about games and helping developers to more easily share their experiences with one another. It is in this language that the students of tomorrow will be taught.

Games (both video and traditional) are tricky to study because they are so multidimensional. There are so many different ways you can approach them. The design and production of games involves aspects of cognitive psychology, computer science, environmental design, and storytelling just to name a few. To really understand what games are, you need to see them from all these points of view.

I always enjoy hearing Raph Koster talk. He's one of the few people I know in the games industry who seems to investigate new subjects that might be relevant to his work, even if it's not immediately obvious why. He forages across wide intellectual landscapes and then returns to share what he's discovered with the rest of us. Not only is he a courageous explorer, he's a diligent mapmaker as well.

In this book Raph does an excellent job of looking at games from a wide variety of perspectives. With the instincts of a designer working in the field, he has filtered out a treasure trove of useful and relevant nuggets from a career's worth of his own research in a variety of related subjects. He then manages to present what he's discovered in a friendly, playful way that makes everything feel like it's falling right into place; it just seems to make perfect sense.

For such a distilled volume of wisdom…I guess I can live with the title.
-*Will Wright*

Will Wright is the Chief Designer for Maxis, the company behind SimCity. He co-founded Maxis with Jeff Braun in 1987. In 1999 he was included in *Entertainment Weekly's* "It List" of "the 100 most creative people in entertainment" as well as *Time Digital's* "Digital 50," a listing of "the most important people shaping technology today."

PROLOGUE: MY GRANDFATHER

My grandfather wanted to know whether I felt proud of what I do. It seemed a reasonable question: there he was, aging and soon to pass away, though at the time I didn't know that; a man who had spent his life as a fire chief, raising six children. One of them followed in his footsteps, became a fire chief himself, and now sells bathtub linings. There's a special education teacher, an architect, a carpenter. Good, solid wholesome professions for good, solid wholesome people. And there I was—making games rather than contributing to society.

I told him that I felt I did contribute. Games aren't just a diversion; they're something valuable and important. And my evidence was right in front of me—my kids, playing tic-tac-toe on the floor.

Watching my kids play and learn through playing had been a revelation for me. Even though my profession was making games, I often felt lost in the complexities of making large modern entertainment products rather than understanding why games are fun and what fun is.

My kids were leading me, without my quite knowing it, toward a theory of fun. And so I told my grandfather, "Yes, this is something worthwhile. I connect people, and I teach people." But as I said it, I didn't really have any evidence to offer.

My kids are learning tic-tac-toe these days.

CHAPTER ONE: WHY WRITE THIS BOOK?

Our kids took to games at a very early age. Games were all around them, and I brought home a crazy amount of them because of my work. I suppose it's no surprise that children model their parents. But my wife and I are also voracious readers, and the kids were resistant to that. Their attraction to games was more instinctive. As babies, they found the game of hide-the-object to be endlessly fascinating, and even now that they are older it elicits an occasional giggle. As babies there was an intentness about their alien gaze as they tried to figure out where the rubber duckie had gone that showed that this game was, for them, in deadly earnest.

Kids are playing everywhere, all the time, and often playing games that we do not quite understand. They play and learn at a ferocious rate. We see the statistics on how many words kids absorb in a day, how rapidly they develop motor control, and how many basic aspects of life they master—aspects that are frankly so subtle that we have even forgotten learning them—and we usually fail to appreciate what an amazing feat this is.

Consider how hard it is to learn a language, and yet children all over the world do it routinely. A *first* language. They are doing it without assigning cognates in their native tongue and without translating in their heads. Recently much attention has been paid to some very special deaf kids in Nicaragua, who have managed to invent a fully functional sign language in just a few generations. Many believe this shows language is built into the brain and that there's something in our wiring that guides us inexorably toward language.

It's fun watching kids learn to play games.

Language is not the only hardwired behavior. As babies move up the developmental ladder, they take part in a variety of instinctual activities. Any parent who has suffered through the "terrible twos" can tell you that it's as if a switch went on in their child's brain, altering their behavior radically. (It lasts longer than just the age of two, by the way—just a friendly warning.)

Kids also move on from certain games as they age. It's been particularly interesting to see my kids outgrow tic-tac-toe—a game I beat them at for years until one day all the matches became draws.

That extended moment when tic-tac-toe ceased to interest them was a moment of great fascination to me. Why, I asked myself, did mastery and understanding come so suddenly? The kids weren't able to tell me that tic-tac-toe is a limited game with optimal strategy. They saw the pattern, but they did not *understand* it, as we think of things.

This isn't unfamiliar to most people. I do many things without fully understanding them, even things I feel I have mastered. I don't need a degree in automotive engineering to drive my car. I don't need to remember the ins and outs of the rules of grammar to speak grammatically in everyday conversation. I don't need to know whether tic-tac-toe is NP-hard or NP-complete to know that it's a dumb game.

decision problems
(yes/no)
yes can be verified

NP

computer science
Non-deterministic
Polynominal time
if NP problem can be solved
using a given problem w
modified input

NP Hard/NP complete
certain classes of
problems are not
solvable in
realistic time

4

They've started to figure out that tic-tac-toe is kind of a dumb game.

I also have plenty of experiences where I stare at something and simply don't get it. I hate to admit it, but my typical reaction is to simply turn away. I feel this way often these days now that there's some (OK, a lot of) gray at my temples. I find myself unable to relate to some of the games that everyone tells me I should be playing. I just can't move the mouse quite as fast as I used to. I'd rather not play than feel that inept, even if the other players are friends of mine.

That's not just me saying, "I can't cut it in Internet play! Damn 14-year-old kids." My reaction isn't mere frustration; it's also got a tinge of boredom. I look at the problem and say, "Well, I could take on the Sisyphean task of trying to match these guys, but frankly, repeated failure is a predictable cycle, and rather boring. I have better things to do with my time."

From everything I hear, this feeling is likely to increase as I age. More and more novel experiences are going to come along, until sometime in 2038 when I'll need the assistance of my smart-ass grandkid to flibber-jibber the frammistan because I won't be able to cope with the newfangled contraptions.

Is this inevitable?

I know how they feel. I'm not a kid anymore, and some days, when I play a game on my computer, it seems like I'm fighting the tide. I quit because I feel inadequate.

When I work on games that are more my speed, I can still crush them (mu ha ha ha). We read all the time about people who play *Scrabble* or other mentally challenging games delaying the onset of Alzheimer's. Surely keeping the mind active keeps it flexible and keeps you young?

Games don't last forever, though. There just comes a point where you say, "You know, I think I've seen most everything that this game has to offer." This happened to me most recently with a typing game I found on the Internet—it was a cute game where I played a diver and sharks were trying to eat me. Each shark had a word on their side, and as I typed the words in, the sharks went belly-up.

Now, I am a terrible formal typist, but I can hunt-and-peck at almost 100 words a minute. This game was fun, but it was also a piece of cake. After level 12 or 14, the game just gave up. It conceded. It said to me, "You know, I've tried every trick I can think of, including words with random punctuation in the middle, words spelled backwards, and not showing you the words until the last minute. So hell with it; from now on, I'll just keep throwing the same challenges at you. But really, you can quit now, because you've seen all I've got."

I took its advice, and quit.

Other times, if I play something I'm good at,
I get really far and do really well, then I get bored.

Games that are too hard kind of bore me, and games that are too easy *also* kind of bore me. As I age, games move from one to the other, just as tic-tac-toe did for our children. Sometimes I play games with people who crush me and afterwards explain kindly, "Well, you see, this is a game about vertices." And I say, "Vertices? I'm putting down pieces on a board!" And they shrug, as if to say I'll never get it.

That's why I decided to tackle the questions of what games are, and what fun is, and why games matter. I knew I'd be going over well-trod ground—a fair amount of psychological literature has been written on developmental behaviors in kids, for example. But the fact is that we don't tend to take games all that seriously.

As I write this a lot of people happen to be exploring these questions. Games, in their digital form, have become big business. We see ads for them on TV, we debate whether or not they make more money than the movie industry (the answer is no, right now, by the way), and we agonize over whether they cause violence in our children. Games are now a major cultural force. The time is ripe for us to dig deeper into the many questions that games raise.

I also find it curious that as parents, we'll insist that kids be given the time to play because it's important to childhood, but that work is deemed far more important later in life. I think work and play aren't all that different, to be honest. And what follows is why I came to that conclusion.

Why are some games fun and other games boring? Why do some games start getting boring after a while, and other games stay fun for a long time?

...oh oh...

CHAPTER TWO: HOW THE BRAIN WORKS

There are a lot of definitions of "game" out there.

There's a field called "game theory," which has something to do with games, a lot to do with psychology, even more to do with math, and not a lot to do with game design. Game theory is about how competitors make optimal choices, and it's mostly used in politics and economics, where it is frequently proven wrong.

Looking up "game" in the dictionary isn't that helpful. Once you leave out the definitions referring to hunting, they wander all over the place. Pastimes or amusements are lumped in with contests. Interestingly, none of the definitions tend to assume that fun is a requirement: amusement or entertainment at best is required.

Those few academics who tried to define "game" have offered up everything from Roger Caillois's "activity which is…voluntary…uncertain, unproductive, governed by rules, make-believe" to Johan Huizinga's "free activity…outside 'ordinary' life…" to Jesper Juul's more contemporary and precise take: "A game is a rule-based formal system with a variable and quantifiable outcome, where different outcomes are assigned different values, the player exerts effort in order to influence the outcome, the player feels attached to the outcome, and the consequences of the activity are optional and negotiable."

None of these help designers find "fun," though.

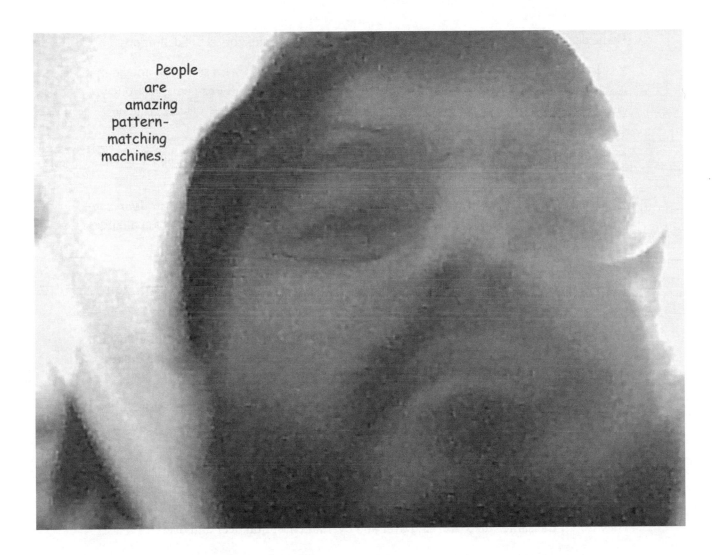

People
are
amazing
pattern-
matching
machines.

Game designers themselves offer a bewildering and often contradictory set of definitions.

- To Chris Crawford, outspoken designer and theorist, games are a subset of entertainment limited to conflicts in which players work to foil each other's goals, just one of many leaves off a tree that includes playthings, toys, challenges, stories, competitions, and a lot more.

- Sid Meier, designer of the classic *Civilization* computer games, gave a classic definition of "a series of meaningful choices."

- Ernest Adams and Andrew Rollings, authors of *Andrew Rollings and Ernest Adams on Game Design,* narrow this further to "one or more causally linked series of challenges in a simulated environment."

- Katie Salen and Eric Zimmerman say in their book *Rules of Play* that a game is "a system in which players engage in an artificial conflict, defined by rules, that results in a quantifiable outcome."

This feels like a quick way to get sucked into quibbling over the classification of individual games. Many simple things can be made complex when you dig into them, but having fun is something so fundamental that surely we can find a more basic concept?

I found my answer in reading about how the brain works. Based on my reading, the human brain is mostly a voracious consumer of patterns, a soft pudgy gray Pac-Man of concepts. Games are just exceptionally tasty patterns to eat up.

When you watch a kid learn, you see there's a recognizable pattern to what they do. They give it a try once—it seems that a kid can't learn by being taught. They have to make mistakes themselves. They push at boundaries to test them and see how far they will bend. They watch the same video over and over and over and over and over and over…

Look at the places we can find a face.

Seeing patterns in how kids learn is evidence of how pattern-driven our brains are. We pattern-seek the process of pattern-seeking! Faces may be the best example. How many times have you seen faces in wood grain, in the patterns in plaster walls, or in the smudges on the sidewalk? A surprisingly large part of the human brain is devoted to seeing faces—when we look at a person's face, a huge amount of brainpower is expended in interpreting it. When we're not looking at someone face-to-face, we often misinterpret what they mean because we lack all the information.

The brain is hardwired for facial recognition just as it is hardwired for language, because faces are incredibly important to how human society works. The capability to see a face in a collection of cartoony lines and interpret remarkably subtle emotions from them is indicative of what the brain does best.

Simply put, the brain is made to fill in blanks. We do this so much we don't even realize we're doing it.

Experts have been telling us for a while now that we're not really "conscious" in the way that we think we are; we do most things on autopilot. But autopilot only works when we have a reasonably accurate picture of the world around us. Our noses really ought to be blocking a lot of our view, but when we cross our eyes, our brains have magically made our nose invisible. What the heck has the brain managed to put in its place? The answer, oddly, is an *assumption*—a reasonable construct based on the input from both eyes and what we have seen before.

Assumptions are what the brain is best at. Some days, I suspect that makes us despair.

Which details

17

There's a whole branch of science dedicated to figuring out how the brain knows what it does. It's already led to a wonderful set of discoveries.

We've learned that if you show someone a movie with a lot of jugglers in it and tell them in advance to count the jugglers, they will probably miss the large pink gorilla in the background, even though it's a somewhat noticeable object. *The brain is good at cutting out the irrelevant.*

We've also found that if you get someone into a hypnotic trance and ask them to describe something, they will often describe much more than if they were asked on the street. *The brain notices a lot more than we think it does.*

We now know that when you ask someone to draw something, they are far more likely to draw the generalized iconic version of the object that they keep in their head than they are to draw the actual object in front of them. In fact, seeing what is actually there with our conscious mind is really hard to do, and most people never learn how to do it! *The brain is actively hiding the real world from us.*

These things fall under the rubric of "cognitive theory," a fancy way of saying "how we think we know what we think we know." Most of them are examples of a concept called "chunking."

When we grasp a pattern, we usually get bored with it and iconify it.

Chunking is something we do all the time.

If I asked you to describe how you got to work in the morning in some detail, you'd list off getting up, stumbling to the bathroom, taking a shower, getting dressed, eating breakfast, leaving the house, and driving to your place of employment. That seems like a good list, until I ask you to walk through exactly how you perform just one of those steps. Consider the step of getting dressed. You'd probably have trouble remembering all the stages. Which do you grab first, tops or bottoms? Do you keep your socks in the top or second drawer? Which leg do you put in your pants first? Which hand touches the button on your shirt first?

Odds are good that you could come to an answer if you thought about it. This is called a morning routine because it *is* routine. You rely on doing these things on autopilot. This whole routine has been "chunked" in your brain, which is why you have to work to recall the individual steps. It's basically a recipe that is burned into your neurons, and you don't "think" about it anymore.

Whatever "thinking" means.

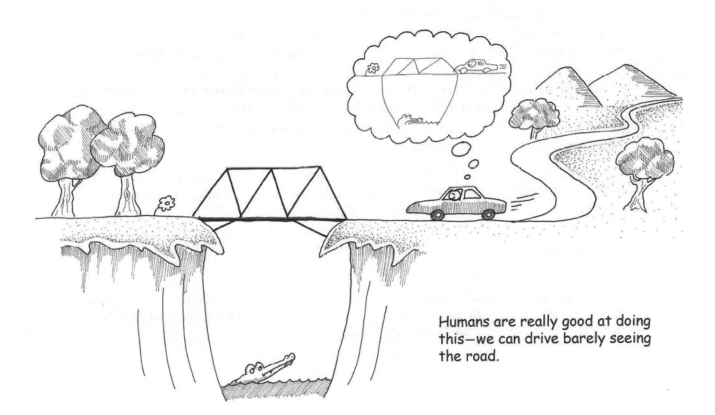

Humans are really good at doing this—we can drive barely seeing the road.

We're usually running on these automatic chunked patterns. In fact, most of what we see is also a chunked pattern. We rarely look at the real world; we instead recognize something we have chunked, and leave it at that. The world could easily be composed of cardboard stand-ins for real objects as far as our brains are concerned. One might argue that the essence of much of art is forcing us to see things as they are rather than as we assume them to be—poems about trees that force us to look at the majesty of bark and the subtlety of leaf, the strength of trunk and the amazing abstractness of the negative space between boughs—those are getting us to ignore the image in our head of "wood, big greenish, whatever" that we take for granted.

why draw

When something in a chunk does not behave as we expect it to, we have problems. It can even get us killed. If cars careen sideways on the road instead of moving forward as we expect them to, we no longer have a rapid response routine. And sadly, conscious thought is really inefficient. If you have to think about what you're doing, you're more liable to screw up. Your reaction times are orders of magnitude slower and odds are good you'll get in a wreck.

How we live in a world of chunking is fascinating. Maybe you're reading this and feeling uncomfortable about whether you're really reading this. But what I really want to talk about is how chunks and routines are built in the first place.

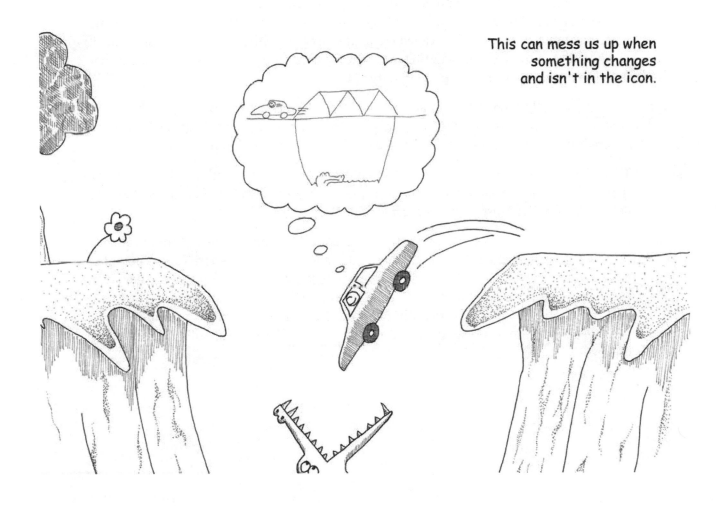

This can mess us up when
something changes
and isn't in the icon.

23

People dislike chaos. We like order—not regimented order, but order with a bit of *texture* or variation to it. For example, there's a long tradition in art history of observing that many paintings use a system of order called *the golden section,* which is basically just a way of dividing up the space on the painting into boxes of different proportions. It turns out that doing so makes the painting appear "prettier" to us.

This isn't exactly a revelation to anyone in the arts. Excess chaos just doesn't have pop appeal. We call it "noise," "ugly," or "formless." My music teacher in college said, "Music is ordered sound and silence." "Ordered" is a pretty important word in that sentence.

There's some highly ordered music that doesn't appeal to most of us either. A lot of folks say that the strain of jazz known as bebop is just noise. But I'm going to offer up an alternate definition of noise: *Noise is any pattern we don't understand.*

Even static has patterns to it. If the little black and white dots are the output of random numbers, they have the pattern of the output of random number generators—a complex pattern, but a pattern nonetheless. If you happen to know the algorithm used to generate the number, and the seed from which the algorithm started, you could exactly replicate that static. There's really next to nothing in the visible universe that is patternless. If we perceive something as noise, it's most likely a failure in ourselves, not a failure in the universe.

When we meet noise,
and fail to see a pattern
in it, we get frustrated,
and give up.

The first time you hear jazz it may sound weird to you, especially if you've been reared on good old-fashioned "three chords and the truth" rock 'n' roll. It'll be "devil music," to borrow a term from countless exasperated parents who railed against their kids' choice of music.

If you get past your initial distaste (which may last only a fraction of a second), you may come to see the patterns inherent in it. For example, you'll spot the flattened fifth that is so important to a jazzy sound. You'll start drumming your fingers to the expected 4/4 beat and find to your dismay that it's actually 7/8 or some other meter. You'll be at sea for a bit, but you may experience a little thrill of delight once you *get it* and experience a moment of discovery, of joy.

If jazz happens to interest you, you'll sink into these patterns and come to expect them. If you get really into it, you may come to feel that a musical style such as alternating-bass folk music is hopelessly "square."

Congratulations, you just chunked up jazz. (Hmm, I hope that doesn't sound too disgusting!)

But once we see a pattern we delight in tracing it and in seeing it reoccur.

That doesn't mean you are done with jazz, though. There's a long way to go between intellectual understanding, intuitive understanding, and grokking something.

"Grok" is a really useful word. Robert Heinlein coined it in his novel *Stranger in a Strange Land*. It means that you understand something so thoroughly that you have become one with it and even *love* it. It's a profound understanding beyond intuition or empathy (though those are required steps on the way).

"Grokking" has a lot in common with what we call "muscle memory." Some writers on cognition describe the brain as functioning on three levels. The first level is what we call conscious thought. It's logical and works on a basically mathematical level, assigning values and making lists. It's kind of slow, even in those genius IQ types. This is the sort of mind we measure when we take IQ tests.

The second level of the brain is really slow. It's integrative, associative, and intuitive. It links things that don't make much sense. This is the part of the brain that packages things up and chunks them. This part of how we think isn't something we can access directly—it doesn't use words. It's also frequently wrong. It's the source of "common sense" which is often self-contradictory ("look before you leap, but he who hesitates is lost"). It's the thing that builds approximations of reality.

We call this "practicing," and the more we do it,

The last kind of thinking is *not* thinking. When you stick your finger in fire, you snatch it back *before* your brain has time to think about it (seriously, it's been measured).

Calling this "muscle memory" is a lie. Muscles don't really have memory. They're just big ol' springs that coil and uncoil when you run electrical current through them. It's really all about nerves. There's a very large part of your body that works based on the *autonomic nervous system,* which is a fancy way of saying that it makes its own decisions. Some of it is stuff you can learn to bring under more conscious control, like your heart rate. Some of it is reflexes, like snatching your fingers out of the fire. And some of it is stuff you train your body to do.

There's an old joke about a crowd gathered at the bottom of a burning building. Up at the top countless people jump from windows to be caught by the firemen. There's one mother who is unwilling to toss her baby to the waiting rescuers. Finally, one guy at the bottom says, "I can catch the kid, ma'am, I'm a famous football player." So the mother tosses the baby to the football player.

It's a bad toss, so he has to run a little ways. He dives to catch the little tyke, and rolls on the ground in a perfect tumble, and finally stands, holding the baby up to a cheering crowd. Everyone is amazed.

Then he drop-kicks the baby.

OK, sick joke aside, it illustrates that we're not just talking about muscle memory, but about whole sets of decisions we make instinctively.

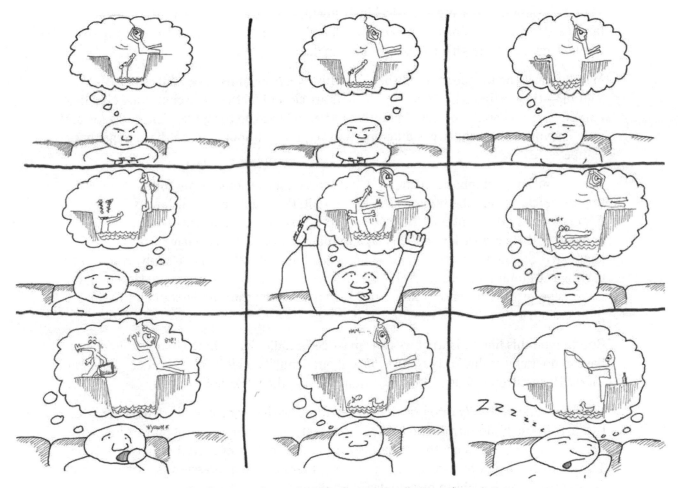

the less we have to think about what we're doing.

Take the example of playing a musical instrument. I play the guitar—mostly acoustic guitar. I've also dabbled in piano and keyboards, and I've had enough musical training that I can fake my way through a banjo or mountain dulcimer.

My wife gave me a mandolin for my birthday this year. Mandolins have a different scale than a guitar—they're tuned like a violin. The frets are closer together. The chords are all different. There are a handful of techniques that just aren't used on the guitar. The notes sustain less. The musical vocabulary is different. And yet, I'm not finding it that hard to get basic competence.

The reason isn't just muscle memory; that just accounts for *some* of my ability to move my fingers quickly along the fingerboard, but not all. For example, the distances I move my fingers are very different and the places I move them to are different too. What is really going on is that because I have been playing guitar for over a decade, I have grokked enough about stringed instruments to create a library of chunked knowledge to apply. When I was playing the guitar all those years, I was also working on more obscure stuff, deepening my knowledge of the intervals between notes, mastering rhythm, understanding harmonic progression.

Building up this library is what we call "practice." Studies have shown that you don't even have to do it physically. You can just *think* about doing it and it'll get you much of the way there. This is strong evidence that the brain is doing the work, not muscles.

When our brain is *really* into practicing something, we'll dream about it. This is the intuitive part of the brain burning neural pathways into our brain, working on turning newly grasped patterns into something that fits within the context of everything else we know. The ultimate goal is to turn it into a routine. Frankly, my impression is that the brain doesn't particularly want to have to deal with it again.

Basically, it's fun to
exercise your brain.

CHAPTER THREE: WHAT GAMES ARE

Which brings us, finally, to games.

If you review those definitions of "game" I presented earlier, you'll see that they have some elements in common. They all present games as if they exist within a world of their own. They describe games as a simulation, a formal system, or as Huizinga put it, a "magic circle" that is disconnected from reality. They all talk about how choices or rules are important, as well as conflict. Finally, a lot of them define games as objects that aren't real, things for pretending with.

But games are very real to me. Games might seem abstracted from reality because they are iconic depictions of patterns in the world. They have more in common with how our brain visualizes things than they do with how reality is actually formed. Since our perception of reality is basically abstractions anyway, I call it a wash.

The pattern depicted may or may not exist in reality. Nobody is claiming that tic-tac-toe is a decent mimicry of warfare, for example. But the rules we perceive—what I'll call the pattern—get processed exactly the same way we process very real things like "fire burns" and "how cars move forward."

Games are puzzles to solve, just like everything else we encounter in life. They are on the same order as learning to drive a car, or picking up the mandolin, or learning your multiplication tables. We learn the underlying patterns, grok them fully, and file them away so that they can be rerun as needed. The only real difference between games and reality is that the stakes are lower with games.

Games are puzzles

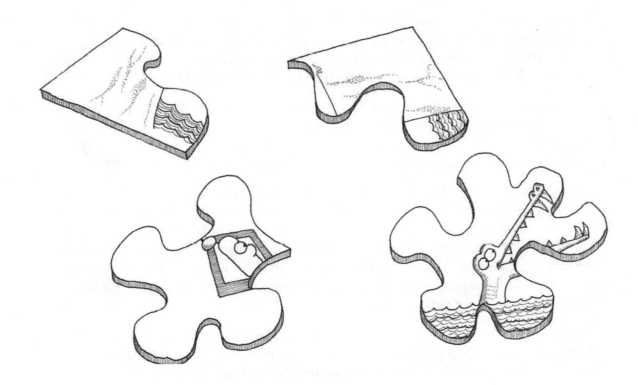

Games are something special and unique. They are concentrated chunks ready for our brains to chew on. Since they are abstracted and iconic, they are readily absorbed. Since they are formal systems, they exclude distracting extra details. Usually, our brains have to do hard work to turn messy reality into something as clear as a game is.

In other words, games serve as very fundamental and powerful learning tools. It's one thing to read in a book that "the map is not the territory" and another to have your armies rolled over by your opponent in a game. When the latter happens, you're *gonna get the point* even if the actual armies aren't marching into your suburban home.

The distinctions between toys and games, or between play and sport, start to seem a bit picky and irrelevant when you look at them in this light. There's been a lot of hay made over how play is non-goal-oriented and games tend to have goals; over how toys are aimed at pointless play rather than being games; about how make-believe is a form of play and not a game.

A game designer might find those distinctions useful because they provide helpful guideposts. But all these things are the same at their most fundamental level. Perhaps this is the reason why language hasn't done a very good job of making distinctions between "play," "game," and "sport." Playing a goal-oriented game involves simply recognizing a particular sort of pattern; playing make-believe is recognizing another one. Both deservedly belong in the same category of "iconified representations of human experience that we can practice with and learn patterns from."

Consider the key difference between something like a book and different kinds of games. A book can do the logical conscious part of the brain pretty well. And really good readers have an ability to slurp that info directly into the subconscious, intuitive mind. But what a book will never be able to do is accelerate the grokking process to the degree that games do, because you cannot practice a pattern and run permutations on it with a book.

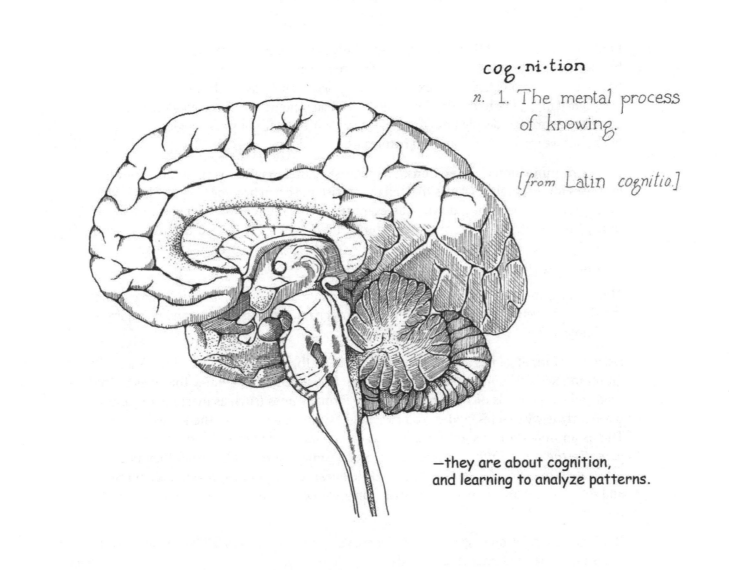

cog·ni·tion

n. 1. The mental process of knowing.

[from Latin *cognitio.*]

—they are about cognition, and learning to analyze patterns.

Linguists have noticed that language obeys fairly strict mathematical rules. For example, humans cannot understand a sentence that is too deeply nested. "The bishop the fireman the mother the football player kicked the baby tossed the baby asked the mother to toss the baby called in the fire to the fire department" is a bad sentence because it violates this rule. The clauses are too deeply nested. We can puzzle it out with our slow logical conscious brain, but we work against our own natures when we do so.

Games run into similar limitations. The biggest of them is their very nature. They are exercises for our brains. Games that fail to exercise the brain become boring. This is why tic-tac-toe ends up falling down—it's exercise, but so limited we don't need to spend much time on it. As we learn more patterns, more novelty is needed to make a game attractive. Practicing can keep a game fresh for a while, but in many cases we'll say, "Enh, I get it, I don't need to practice this task," and we'll move on.

Almost all games fall prey to this. They are limited formal systems. If you keep playing them, you'll eventually grok them. In that sense, games are disposable, and boredom is inevitable.

Extremely formal games are more susceptible to mathematical analysis, which is a limitation in itself. We don't think that we can drive just because we know the rules of the road and the controls of a car, but extremely formal games (such as most board games) have fairly few variables, and so you can often extrapolate out from the known rule set. This is an important insight for game designers: *the more formally constructed your game is, the more limited it will be.* To make games more long-lasting, they need to integrate more variables (and less predictable ones) such as human psychology, physics, and so on. These are elements that arise from outside the game's rules and from outside the "magic circle."

(If it's any consolation to games, that's where game theory tends to fall down too—psych tends not to be that amenable to math.)

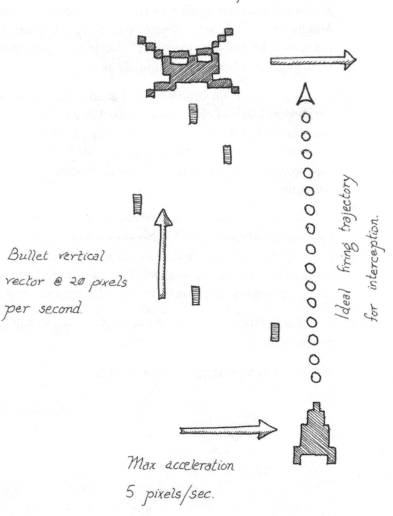

Constant motion @ 3 pixels / second.

Ideal firing trajectory for interception.

When you're playing a game, it exercises your brain,

Bullet vertical vector @ 20 pixels per second.

Max acceleration 5 pixels/sec.

This finally brings us to the title of the book and the fundamental question: What is fun?

If you dig into the origins of the word, it comes either from *"fonne,"* which is "fool" in Middle English, or from *"fonn,"* which means "pleasure" in Gaelic. Either way, fun is defined as "a source of enjoyment." This can happen via physical stimuli, aesthetic appreciation, or direct chemical manipulation.

Fun is all about our brains feeling good—the release of endorphins into our system. The various cocktails of chemicals released in different ways are basically all the same. Science has shown that the pleasurable chills that we get down the spine after exceptionally powerful music or a really great book are caused by the same sorts of chemicals we get when we have cocaine, an orgasm, or chocolate. Basically, our brains are on drugs pretty much all the time.

One of the subtlest releases of chemicals is at that moment of triumph when we learn something or master a task. This almost always causes us to break out into a smile. After all, it is important to the survival of the species that we learn—therefore our bodies reward us for it with moments of pleasure. There are many ways we find fun in games, and I will talk about the others. But this is the most important.

Fun from games arises out of mastery. It arises out of comprehension. It is the act of solving puzzles that makes games fun.

In other words, with games, learning is the drug.

but you'll only play it until you master the pattern.

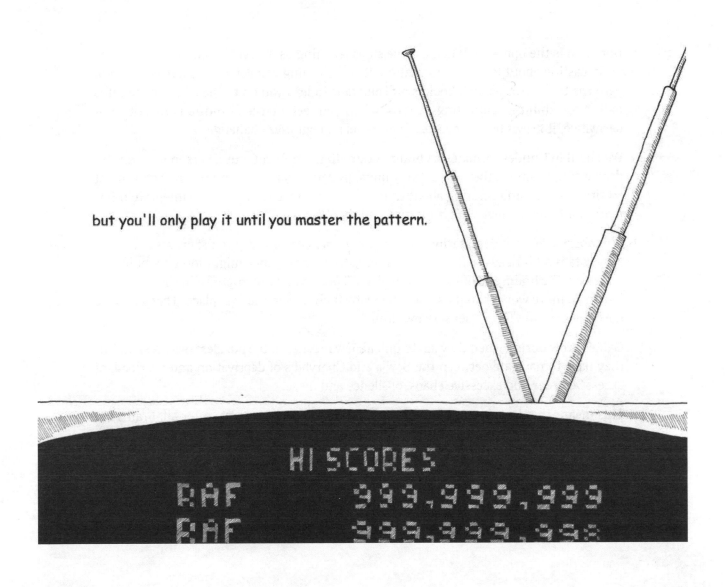

41

Boredom is the opposite. When a game stops teaching us, we feel bored. Boredom is the brain casting about for new information. It is the feeling you get when there are no new patterns to absorb. When a book is dull and fails to lead you on to the next chapter, it is failing to exhibit a captivating pattern. When you feel a piece of music is repetitive or derivative, it grows boring because it presents no cognitive challenge.

We shouldn't underestimate the brain's desire to learn. If you put a person in a sensory deprivation chamber, they will get very unhappy very quickly. The brain craves stimuli. At all times, the brain is casting about trying to learn something, trying to integrate information into its worldview. It is insatiable in that way.

This *doesn't* mean it necessarily craves new *experiences*—mostly, it just craves new *data*. New data is all it needs to flesh out a pattern. A new experience might force a whole new system on the brain, and often the brain doesn't *like* that. It's disruptive. The brain doesn't like to do more work than it has to. That's why it chunks in the first place. That's why we have the opposite term, "sensory overload."

Games grow boring when they fail to unfold new niceties in the puzzles they present. But they have to navigate between the Scylla and Charybdis of deprivation and overload, of excessive order and excessive chaos, of silence and noise.

This means that boredom might not wait until the end of the game. After all, brains are *really* good at pattern-matching and dismissing noise and silence.

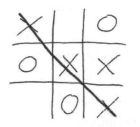 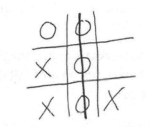 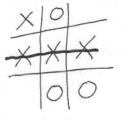 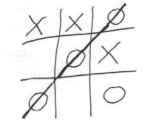

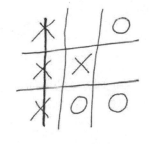 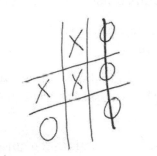 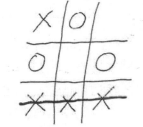

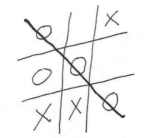 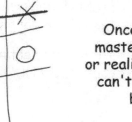

Once you've
mastered it—
or realized you
can't get any
better—

Here are some ways in which boredom might strike, killing the pleasurable learning experience that games are supposed to provide:

- The player might grok how the game works from just the first five minutes, and then the game will be dismissed as trivial, just as an adult dismisses tic-tac-toe. "Too easy," might be the remark the player makes.

- The player might grok that there's a ton of depth to the possible permutations in a game but conclude that these permutations are below their level of interest— sort of like saying, "Yeah, there's a ton of depth in baseball, but memorizing the RBI stats for the past 20 years is not all that useful to me."

- The player might fail to see any patterns whatsoever, and nothing is more boring than noise. "This is too hard."

- The pacing of the unveiling of variations in the pattern might be too slow, in which case the game may be dismissed as trivial too early. "This is too easy now—it's repetitive."

- The game might also unveil the variations too quickly, which then leads to players losing control of the pattern and giving up because it looks like noise again. "This got too hard too fast," they'll say.

- The player might master everything in the pattern. They have exhausted the fun, consumed it all. "I beat it."

the game becomes boring.

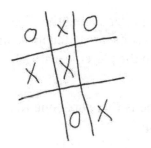

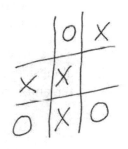

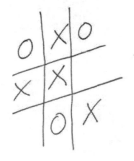

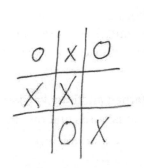

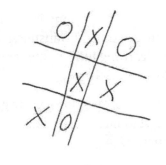

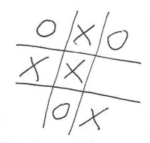

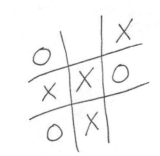

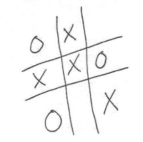

Any of these will result in the player stating that they are bored. In reality, some of these are boredom+frustration, and some are boredom+triumph, and so on. If your goal is to keep things fun (read as "keep the player learning"), boredom is always the signal to let you know you have failed.

The definition of a good game is therefore "one that teaches everything it has to offer before the player stops playing."

That's what games are, in the end. Teachers. Fun is just another word for learning.

One wonders, then, why learning is so damn boring to so many people. It's almost certainly because the method of transmission is wrong. We praise good teachers by saying that they "make learning fun." Games are very good teachers... of something. The question is, what do they teach?

Either way, I have an answer for my late grandfather, and it looks like what I do fits right alongside the upstanding professions of my various aunts and uncles. Fireman, carpenter, and... teacher.

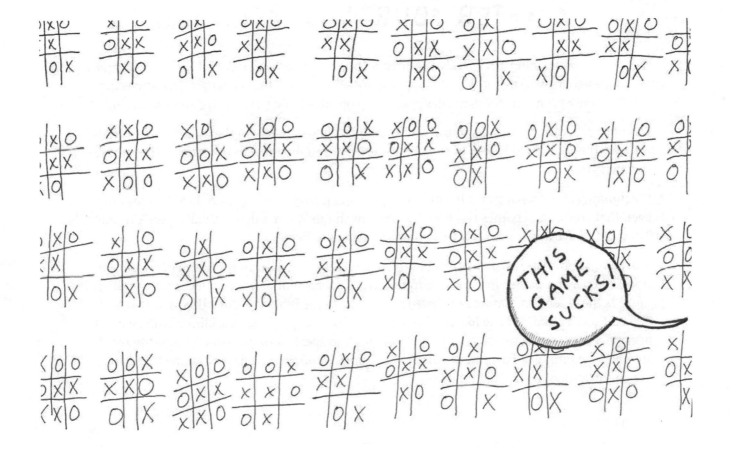

Basically, all games are edutainment.

CHAPTER FOUR: WHAT GAMES TEACH US

Formal training isn't really required to become a game designer. Most of the game designers working professionally today are self-taught. That is changing rapidly as university programs for game designers crop up all around the country and the world.

I went to school to be a writer, mostly. I believe really passionately in the importance of writing and the incredible power of fiction. We learn through stories; we become who we are through stories.

My thinking about what fun is led me to similar conclusions about games. I can't deny, however, that stories and games teach really different things. Games don't usually have a moral. They don't have a theme in the sense that a novel has a theme.

but do have a visual theme

The population that uses games most effectively is the young. Certainly folks in every generation keep playing games into old age (pinochle, anyone?), but as we get older we view them more as the exception. Games are viewed as frivolity. In the Bible in 1 Corinthians, we are told, "When I was a child, I spoke like a child, I thought like a child, I reasoned like a child; when I became a man, I gave up childish ways." But children speak honestly—sometimes too much so. Their reasoning is far from impaired—it is simply inexperienced. We assume that games are childish ways, but is that really so?

This shouldn't surprise us—after all,
the young of all species play.

We don't actually put away the notion of "having fun," near as I can tell. We migrate it into other contexts. Many claim that work is fun, for example (me included). Just getting together with friends can be enough to give us the little burst of endorphins we crave.

We also don't put aside the notion of constructing abstract models of reality in order to practice with them. We practice our speeches in front of mirrors, run fire drills, go through training programs, and role-play in therapy sessions. There are games all around us. We just don't call them that.

As we age, we think that things are more serious and that we must leave frivolous things behind. Is that a value judgment on games or is it a value judgment on the content of a given game? Do we avoid the notion of fun because we view the content of the fire drill as being of greater import?

Most importantly—would fire drills be more effective if they were fun activities?

With age, some games turn serious.

If games are essentially models of reality, then the things that games teach us must reflect on reality.

My first thought was that games are models of hypothetical realities since they often bear no resemblance to any reality I know.

As I looked deeper, though, I found that even whacked-out abstract games do reflect underlying reality. The guys who told me these games were all about vertices were correct. Since formal rule sets are basically mathematical constructs, they always end up reflecting forms of mathematical truth, at the very least. (Formal rule sets are the basis for most games, but not all—there are classes of games with informal rule sets, but you can bet that the little girls will cry "no fair" when someone violates an unstated assumption in their tea party.)

Sadly, reflecting mathematical structures is also the only thing many games do.

The real-life challenges that games prepare us for are almost exclusively ones based on the calculation of odds. They teach us how to predict events. A huge number of games simulate forms of combat. Even games ostensibly about building are usually framed competitively.

Given that we're basically hierarchical and strongly tribal primates, it's not surprising that most of the basic lessons we are taught by our early childhood play are about power and status. Think about how important these lessons still are within society, regardless of your particular culture. Games almost always teach us tools for being the top monkey.

The very phrase
"it's just a game"
implies that
playing a game is
a form of
PRACTICE
for a real-life
challenge.

*playing?
or
training?*

53

Games also teach us how to examine the environment, or space, around us. From games where we fit together odd shapes to games where we learn to see the invisible lines of power projection across a grid, much effort is spent in teaching us about territory. That is what tic-tac-toe is essentially all about.

Spatial relationships are, of course, critically important to us. Some animals might be able to navigate the world using the Earth's magnetic field, but not us. Instead, we use maps and we use them to map all sorts of things, not just space. Learning to interpret symbols on a map, assess distance, assess risk, and remember caches must have been a critically important survival skill when we were nomadic tribesmen. But we also map things like temperature. We map social relationships (as graphs of edges and vertices, in fact). We map things over time.

Examining space also fits into our nature as toolmakers. We learn how things fit together. We often abstract this a lot—we play games where things fit together not only physically, but conceptually as well. By playing games of classification and taxonomy, we extend mental maps of relationships between objects. With these maps, we can extrapolate behaviors of these objects.

Most games incorporate some element of spatial reasoning. The space may be a Cartesian coordinate space, or it may be a directed conceptual graph, but it's all the same thing in the end (as a mathematician will tell you). Classifying, collating, and exercising power over the contents of a space is one of the fundamental lessons of all kinds of gameplay.

Some games teach spatial relationships.

Exploring conceptual spaces is critical to our success in life. Merely understanding a space and how the rules make it work isn't enough, though. We also need to understand how it will react to change to exercise power over it. This is why games progress over time. There are no games that take just one turn.

Let's consider so-called "games of chance" that use a six-sided die. Here we have a possibility space—values labeled 1 through 6. If you roll dice against someone, the game you are playing might seem to end very quickly. You also might feel you don't have much control over the outcome. You might think an activity like this shouldn't be called a game. It certainly seems like a game you can play in one turn.

But I suggest gambling games like this are actually designed to teach us about odds. You don't just play for one turn, and with each turn you try to learn more about how odds work. (Unfortunately, you prove you didn't learn the lesson—especially if you are gambling for money.) We know from experiments that probability is something our brains have serious trouble grasping.

Exploring a possibility space is the only way to learn about it. Most games repeatedly throw evolving spaces at you so that you can explore the recurrence of symbols within them. A modern video game will give you tools to navigate a complicated space, and when you finish, the game will give you another space, and another, and another.

Some of the really important parts of exploration involve memory. A huge number of games involve recalling and managing very long and complex chains of information. (Think about counting cards in blackjack or playing competitive dominoes.) Many games involve thoroughly exploring the possibility space as part of their victory condition.

Some games teach you to explore.

In the end, most games have something to do with power. Even the innocuous games of childhood tend to have violence lurking in their heart of hearts. Playing "house" is about jockeying for social status. It is richly multileveled, as kids position themselves in authority or not over other kids. They play-act at using the authority that their parents exercise over them. (There's this idealized picture of girls as being all sweetness and light, but there are few more viciously status-driven groups on earth.)

Consider the games that get all the attention lately: shooters, fighting games, and war games. They are not subtle about their love of power. The gap between playing these games and cops and robbers is small as far as the players are concerned. They are all about reaction times, tactical awareness, assessing the weaknesses of an opponent, and judging when to strike. Just as my playing guitar was in fact preparing me for playing mandolin by teaching me skills beyond basic guitar fretting, these games teach many skills that are relevant in a corporate setting. We pay attention to the obvious nature of a particular game and we miss the subtler point; be it cops and robbers or *CounterStrike*, the real lessons are about team-work and not about aiming.

Think about it; teamwork is a far deadlier tool than sharpshooting.

Some games teach you how to aim precisely.

Many games, particularly those that have evolved into the classic Olympian sports, can be directly traced back to the needs of primitive humans to survive under very difficult conditions. Many things we have fun at doing are in fact training us to be better cavemen. We learn skills that are antiquated. Most folks never need to shoot something with an arrow to eat, and we run marathons or other long races mostly to raise funds for charities.

Nonetheless, we have fun mostly to improve our life skills. And while there may be something deep in our reptile brains that wants us to continue practicing aiming or sentry-posting, we do in fact evolve games that are more suited to our modern lives.

From playing
cops and robbers
to
playing house,
play is about
learning life skills.

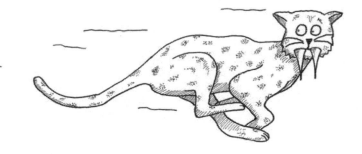

For example, there are many games in my collection <u>that relate to network building.</u> Building railway lines or aqueducts wasn't exactly a caveman activity. As humans have evolved, we've changed around our games. In early versions of chess, queens weren't nearly as powerful a piece as they are today.

Many games have become obsolete and are no longer played. Grain harvesting used to be a really big deal, but it isn't now. You can't find many games about farming on the market as a result. In general, the level of mathematical sophistication required by games has risen dramatically over the course of human history as common people learned how to do sums. Word games were once restricted to the elite, but today they are enjoyed by the masses.

Games do adapt, but perhaps not as fast as we might wish, since almost all of these games are still, at their core, about the same activities even though they may involve different skill sets.

Some of which might be useful, and some of which

might not.

In some ways games can be compared to music (which is even more mathematically driven). Music excels at conveying only a few things—emotion being paramount among them. Games do very well at active verbs: controlling, projecting, surrounding, matching, remembering, counting, and so on. Games are also very good at quantification.

By contrast, literature can tackle all of the above and more. Over time, language-based media have tackled increasingly broader subjects.

Games are also capable of modeling situations of greater richness and complexity. Games like *Diplomacy* are evidence that remarkably subtle interactions can be modeled within the confines of a rule set, and traditional role-playing can reach the same heights as literature in the right hands. But it is an uphill battle nonetheless, simply because games are at their core about teaching us survival skills. As we all know, when you're worried about subsistence and survival, more refined things tend to fall by the wayside.

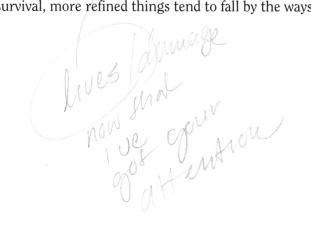

aiming

timing

hunting

territory

projecting power

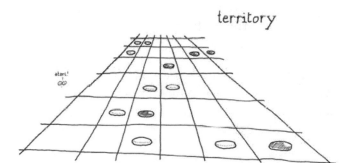

When you get right down to it, most games are teaching us about only a few things,

It's worth asking ourselves what skills are more commonly needed today. Games should be evolving toward teaching us those skills.

The entire spread of games for children is fairly limited and hasn't changed much. The basic skills needed by children are the same. Perhaps we need a few more games about changing TV channels, but that's about it. Adults, on the other hand, could use new games that teach more relevant skills. Most of us no longer hunt our own food and we no longer live in danger every moment of our lives. It's still valuable to train ourselves in some of the caveman traits, but we need to adapt.

Some traits are relevant but need to change because conditions have changed. Interesting research has been done into what people find disgusting, for example. Disgust is a survival trait that points us away from grayish-green, mucousy, slimy things. It does so because that was the most likely vector for illness.

Today it might be the electric blue fluid that is the real risk—don't drink any drain cleaner—and we have no inborn revulsion toward it. In fact, it's made electric blue to make it seem aseptic and clean. That's a case where we should supplement our instincts with training, since I doubt there's anything I can drink under my kitchen sink.

and mostly,
they are things
that were useful to us
when our species
was first evolving.

Some of the new patterns we need to learn in our brave new world run contrary to our instinctive behaviors. For example, humans are tribal creatures. We not only fall readily into groups run by outsize personalities, but we'll often subsume our better judgment in doing so. We also seem to have an inbred dislike of groups not our own. It is very easy to get humans to regard a different tribe as less than human, particularly if they look or act differently in some way.

Maybe this was a survival trait at one time, but it's not now. Our world grows ever more interdependent; if a currency collapse occurs on the other side of the world, the price of milk at our local grocery could be affected. A lack of empathy and understanding of different tribes and xenophobic hatred can really work against us.

Most games encourage demonizing the opponent, teaching a sort of ruthlessness that is a proven survival trait. But these days, we're less likely to need or want the scorched-earth victory. Can we create games that instead offer us greater insight into how the modern world works?

If I were to identify other basic human traits that games currently tend to reinforce and that may be obsolete legacies of our heritage, I might call out traits like

- Blind obedience to leaders and cultism

- Rigid hierarchies

- Binary thinking

- The use of force to resolve problems

- Like seeking like, and its converse, xenophobia

group discuss is this still true when date was given

It's not surprising that games boil down to so few basic patterns. After all, as cavemen, we needed to be able to recognize food or danger under widely varying circumstances.

69

For better or worse, games have been ringing changes on the same few subjects. There's probably something deep in the reptile brain that is deeply satisfied by jumping puzzles, but you'd think that by now we would have jumped over everything in every possible way.

When I first started playing games, everything was tile based, meaning that you moved in discrete squares, as if you were popping from tile to tile on a tiled floor. Nowadays you move in a much freer way, but what has changed is the fidelity of the simulation, not what we're simulating. The skills required are perhaps closer to being what they are in reality, and yet an improvement in the simulation of crossing a pond full of alligators is not necessarily something relevant.

The mathematical field of studying shape and the way in which apparent shapes can change but remain the same is called *topology*. It can be helpful to think of games in terms of their topology.

Early platform games followed a few basic gameplay paradigms.

- **"Get to the other side" games**. *Frogger, Donkey Kong, Kangaroo*. These are not really very dissimilar. Some of these featured a time limit, some didn't.

- **"Visit every location" games**. Probably the best known early platformer like this was *Miner 2049er*, *Pac-Man* and *Q*Bert* also made use of this mechanic. The most cerebral of these were probably *Lode Runner* and *Apple Panic,* where the map traversal could get very complex given the fact that you could modify the map to a degree.

Games started to meld these two styles, then they added scrolling environments. Eventually designers added playing in 3-D on rails and finally made the leap to true 3-D with *Mario 64*.

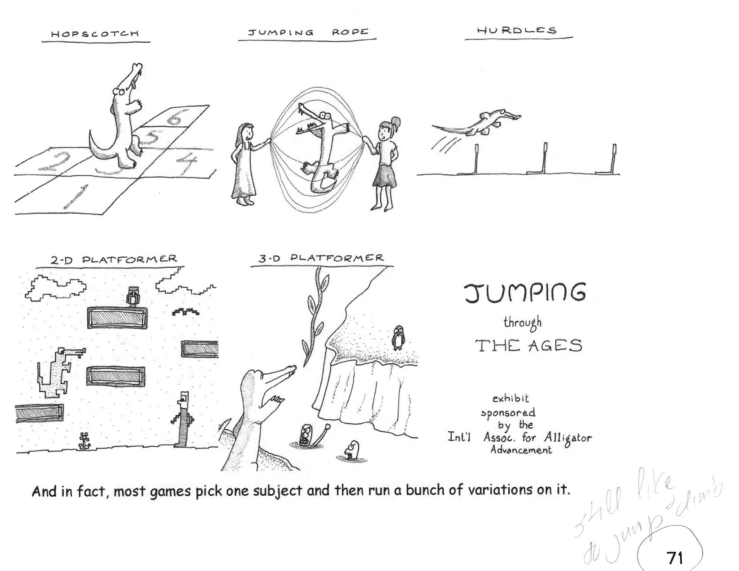

HOPSCOTCH   JUMPING ROPE   HURDLES

2-D PLATFORMER   3-D PLATFORMER

JUMPING

through

THE AGES

exhibit
sponsored
by the
Int'l Assoc. for Alligator
Advancement

And in fact, most games pick one subject and then run a bunch of variations on it.

A modern platformer makes use of all of these dimensions:

- "Get to the other side" is still the basic paradigm.

- "Visit all the map" is handled by a "secrets" system.

- Time limits add another dimension of challenge.

Since the original *Donkey Kong,* players have been able to pick up a hammer to use as a weapon. One of the commonest signs of incremental innovation in game design is designers simply adding more of a given element rather than adding a new element. Hence, today we have a bewildering array of weapons.

Platformers have now covered all the dimensions. They have started pulling in elements of racing and flying games and fighters and shooters. They have built in secret discovery and time limits and power-ups. Recent games have included more robust stories and even elements from role-playing games. Are there more dimensions on which to expand?

Going from *Pong* to a modern tennis game is not so large a leap. How odd that we've ended up in the recursive pattern of making games that model other games—it suggests that there's something that the real-life sport of tennis can teach that doesn't require running around on a court in a white outfit now. Nonetheless, rather than teaching the skill of hurling rocks and judging trajectories, it would be nice if games instead taught things like whether or not the price of oil is going to rise in response to signing or not signing a global warming treaty.

This may sound bleak, but in fact, it's not. The skills needed around a meeting room table and the skills needed at the tribal council are not so different, after all. There are whole genres of game that are about husbandry, resource management, logistics, and negotiation. If anything, the question to ask might be why the most popular games are the ones that teach obsolete skills while the more sophisticated ones that teach subtler skills tend to reach smaller markets.

Just like variations on a theme in music,
these are basically training to recognize
a pattern in a variety of situations.

A lot of it can probably be traced to visceral appeal. Remember, we live most of our lives in the unconscious. Action games let us stay there, whereas games that demand careful consideration of logistics might require logical, conscious thought. So we ring changes on old, often irrelevant challenges because, frankly, it's easier.

We've evolved exquisite sensitivity to visceral challenges. A survey of games featuring jumping found that the games with the "best controls" all shared an important characteristic: when you hit the jump button, the character on screen spent almost exactly the same amount of time in the air. Games with "bad controls" violated this unspoken assumption. I'm pretty sure that if we went looking, we'd find that good jumping games have been unscientifically adhering to this unspoken rule for a couple of decades, without ever noticing its existence.

That's hardly the only case of our adjusting our work to better target the unconscious mind. A very common feature of action games, for example, is to push you through a task faster and faster. This is purely intended to address the visceral reaction and the autonomic nervous system. When you learn any physical skill, you are told to do it slowly at first and slowly increase the speed as you master the task. The reason is that developing speed without precision is not all that useful. Going slow lets you practice the precision first, make it unconscious, and then work on the speed.

You don't tend to see "time attack" modes in strategy games, for this same reason. The tasks in the strategic games are not about automatic responses, and therefore the training to execute at reflex levels of speed would be misguided. (If anything, a good strategy game will teach you not to get too familiar with the situation and will keep you on your toes.)

This whole approach is intended for learning by rote. When I was a kid, I had a game for the Atari 2600 console called *Laser Blast*. I got to the point where I could get a million points at the maximum difficulty setting without ever dying. With my eyes closed. This is the same sort of training that we put our militaries through—the training of rote and reflex. It's not a very *adaptable* mode of training, but it is desirable in many cases.

Sometimes we ask you to do a task faster.

A more interesting tactic that applies to a wider range of games is asking the player to be thorough. This is a broader survival skill. It requires patience, and a certain enjoyment of discovery. It also works against our inclination to work directly on the final goal.

In many games, you are asked to find "secrets" or to explore an area completely. This teaches many interesting things, such as considering a problem from all angles, making sure that you should make sure you have all the information before you make a decision, and thoroughness is often better than speed. Not to denigrate training by rote and reflex, but this is a much subtler and interesting set of skills to teach, and one that is more widely applicable to the modern world.

Games have these characteristics:

- They present us with models of real things—often highly abstracted.

- They are generally quantified or even *quantied* models.

- They primarily teach us things that we can absorb into the unconscious as opposed to things designed to be tackled by the conscious, logical mind.

- They mostly teach us things that are fairly primitive behaviors, but they don't *have* to.

Seen in this light, it's not surprising that the evolution of the modern video game can largely be explained in terms of topology. Each generation of game can be described by a relatively minute alteration in the shape of the play space. For example, there have only really been around five fighting games in all of videogaming history. Significant advances have been limited to a few features like movement on a plane, movement in 3-D, and the addition of "combos" or sequences of moves.

This is not to say that many of the classic fighting games didn't bring significant incremental advances. Of course they did. But did they effectively "add another hole to the donut"?

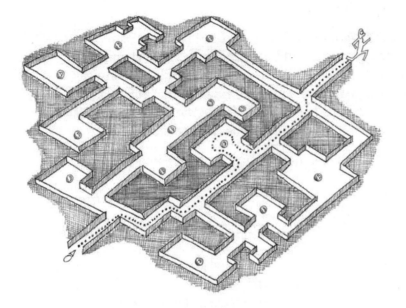

Sometimes we ask you to do it more thoroughly.

Consider the evolution of the 2-D shooter or "shmup." *Space Invaders* offered a single screen with enemies that marched predictably. After that came *Galaxian,* which had no defenses and enemies that attacked a bit more aggressively.

Simple topological variants then ensued: *Gyruss* and *Tempest* are just *Galaxian* in a circle. *Gorf* and others added scrolling and also had an end boss and stages that changed in nature as you progressed. *Zaxxon* added verticality, which was then quickly thrown away in the development of the genre. *Centipede* gave you some room to maneuver at the bottom, and a charming setting, but isn't really that different from *Galaxian. Asteroids* is an inverted circle: you're in the middle, and the enemies come from outside.

Galaga was probably the most influential of all of these because it added bonus levels and the power-up, a concept that has become standard in every shmup since. *Xevious* and *Vanguard* added alternate modes of fire (bombs and firing in other directions). *Robotron* and *Defender* are special cases. Both have the element of rescuing. This has been pretty much abandoned today (sadly—though *Choplifter* was a wonderful sidetrack there).

Now, I don't know what the first 2-D shooter to have power-ups and scrolling and bosses at the end of stages was, but a case can be made that there hasn't been a topologically different 2-D shooter since. Unsurprisingly, the shooter genre has stagnated and lost market share. After all, we learned that mechanic a long time ago, and everything since has been learning patterns that we *know* to be artificial and unlikely to be repeated anywhere.

This offers a possible algorithm for innovation: *find a new dimension to add to the gameplay*. We saw this in the way that puzzle games evolved after *Tetris*: people started trying to do it with hexagons, with three dimensions, and eventually, pattern matching of colors became the thing that replaced spatial analysis. If we really wanted to innovate on puzzle games, how about exploring puzzle games based on time rather than space, for example?

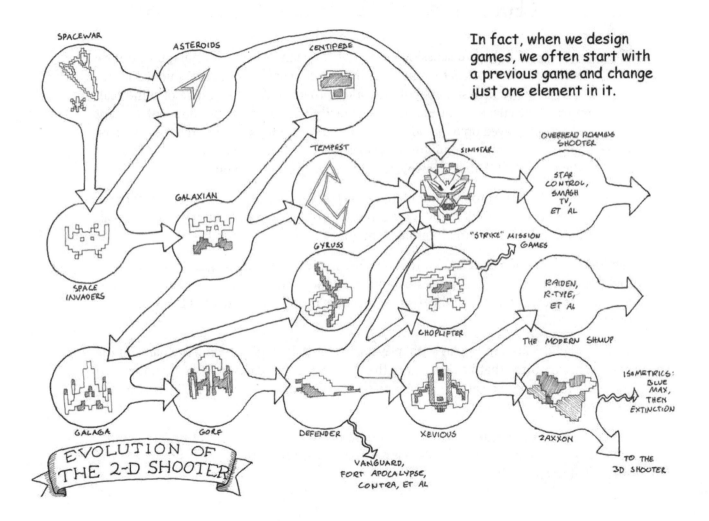

In fact, when we design games, we often start with a previous game and change just one element in it.

SPACEWAR

ASTEROIDS

CENTIPEDE

TEMPEST

SIMISTAR

OVERHEAD ROAMING SHOOTER

STAR CONTROL, SMASH TV, ET AL

GALAXIAN

GYRUSS

"STRIKE" MISSION GAMES

SPACE INVADERS

CHOPLIFTER

RAIDEN, R-TYPE, ET AL

THE MODERN SHMUP

GALAGA

GORF

DEFENDER

XEVIOUS

ZAXXON

ISOMETRICS: BLUE MAX, THEN EXTINCTION

TO THE 3D SHOOTER

EVOLUTION OF THE 2-D SHOOTER

VANGUARD, FORT APOCALYPSE, CONTRA, ET AL

CHAPTER FIVE: What Games Aren't

Until now, I've been discussing formal game design—abstract simulations. But we rarely see truly abstract simulations in games. People tend to dress up game systems with some fiction. Designers put artwork on them that is suggestive of some real-world context. Take checkers for example—abstractly, it's a board game about entrapment and forced action, played on a diamond-shaped grid. When we say "king me" in checkers, we're adding a subtle bit of fiction to the game; suddenly it has acquired feudal overtones and a medieval context. Usually, the pieces have a crown embossed on them.

This is similar to word problems in math class. The fiction serves two purposes: it trains you to see past it to the underlying math problem, and it also trains you to recognize real-world situations where that math problem might be lurking.

Games in general tend to be like word problems. You won't find many games that are pure unclothed abstractions. Most games have more in common with chess or checkers—they provide some level of misdirection. Usually there are metaphors for what is going on in the game.

choice

While metaphors are fun to play with, players can basically ignore them. The name of the unique checker piece that has made it to the other side is basically irrelevant, mathematically speaking. We could call the regular pieces chickens and the crowned ones wolves and the game would not change one whit.

Games, by the very nature of what they teach, push toward this sort of understanding. Since they are about teaching underlying patterns, they train their players to ignore the fiction that wraps the patterns.

but can 'talk' about it more
art
fiction
mood work etc

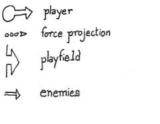

player

force projection

playfield

enemies

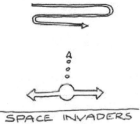

SPACE INVADERS

GALAXIAN

TEMPEST

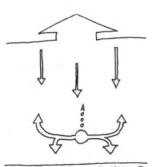

SCROLLING SH'MUP

Games are largely about
getting people to see
past the variations
and look instead at
the underlying patterns.
Because of this, gamers
are very good at seeing
past fiction.

Back in 1976, a company called Exidy scored a first in video game history: its game *Deathrace* was taken off the market because of public concerns about the game's violent nature. *Deathrace* was loosely based on a movie called *Deathrace 2000*. The premise involved driving a car to run over pedestrians for points.

Mechanically, *Deathrace* was the same as any other game that involved catching objects moving around the screen. If you looked at this game today, however, with its crude pixilated graphics and its tiny iconic people, you wouldn't be particularly shocked. After all, countless other gore-fests have come along that make the game look quaint.

I don't think debates about the suitability of violence in the media will disappear. Much evidence shows that media have some effect on how we act. If media didn't have an effect, we wouldn't spend so much effort on using it as teaching tools. But evidence also shows that media aren't mind-control devices (of course they aren't, or else we'd all behave like the people we read about in the children's stories we read in elementary school).

Gamers, however, have always viewed this issue with some perplexity. When they defend their beloved games, they use one of the most self-defeating rallying cries in history: "It's only a game!"

In the wake of school shootings and ex-military people decrying first-person shooters as "murder simulators," this argument doesn't carry a lot of weight. Academics who disagree with the portrayal of games as damaging to children tend to muster learned arguments about privileged spaces and magic circles. Much of the public dismisses these arguments as coming from an ivory tower.

But there's a very good reason why the gamers are incredulous.

This is why gamers are dismissive of the ethical implications of games—

they don't see "get a blowjob from a hooker, then run her over."

Remember, games train us to see underlying mathematical patterns. The fact that I can describe *Deathrace* as being a game about picking up objects on a two-dimensional playing field is evidence that its "dressing" is largely irrelevant to what the game is about at its core. As you get more into a game, you'll most likely cut to the chase and examine the true underpinnings of the game, just as a music aficionado can cut past the lyrical content of different types of Latin music and determine whether a given song is a *cumbia* or a *marinera* or a *salsa*.

Running over pedestrians, killing people, fighting terrorists, and eating dots while running from ghosts are all just stage settings, convenient metaphors for what a game is actually teaching. *Deathrace* does not teach you to run over pedestrians any more than *Pac-Man* teaches you to eat dots and be scared of ghosts.

None of this is to minimize the fact that *Deathrace does* involve running over pedestrians and squishing them into little tombstone icons. That's there, for sure, and it's kind of reprehensible. It's not a great setting or staging for the game, but it's also not what the game is really about.

Learning to see that division is important to our understanding of games, and I'll touch on it at greater length later. For now, suffice it to say that the part of games that is *least* understood is the formal abstract system portion of it, the mathematical part of it, the chunky part of it. Attacks on other aspects of games are likely to miss the key point—at their core games need to develop this formal aspect of themselves in order to improve.

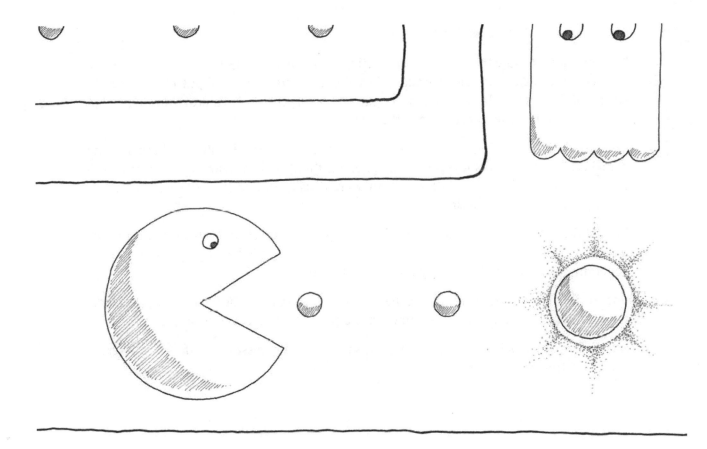

They see a power-up.

Alas, that isn't what we tend to focus on.

The commonest route these days for developing games involves grafting a story onto them. But most video game developers take a (usually mediocre) story and put little game obstacles all through it. It's as if we are requiring the player to solve a crossword puzzle in order to turn the page to get more of the novel.

Classd would argue this

By and large, people don't play games because of the stories. The stories that wrap the games are usually side dishes for the brain. For one thing, it's damn rare to see a game story written by an actual writer. As a result, they are usually around the high-school level of literary sophistication at best.

For another, since the games are generally about power, control, and those other primitive things, the stories tend to be so as well. This means they tend to be power fantasies. That's generally considered to be a pretty juvenile sort of story.

The stories in most video games serve the same purpose as calling the über-checker a "king." It adds interesting shading to the game but the game at its core is unchanged.

Remember—my background is as a writer, so this actually pisses me off. Story deserves better treatment than that.

Story, setting, and backplot in games are nothing more than an attempt to give a side dish to the brain while it completes its challenges—sometimes, the hope is that it makes up for an otherwise unremarkable game.

Games are not stories. It is interesting to make the comparison, though:

- Games tend to be <u>experiential</u> teaching. Stories teach <u>vicariously.</u>

- Games are good at <u>objectification.</u> Stories are good at <u>empathy.</u>

- Games tend to quantize, reduce, and classify. Stories tend to blur, deepen, and make subtle distinctions.

- Games are external—<u>they are about people's actions.</u> Stories (good ones, anyway) are <u>internal</u>—they are about people's emotions and thoughts.

In both cases, when they are good, you can come back to them repeatedly and keep learning something new. But <u>we never speak of fully mastering a good story.</u>

I don't think anyone would quarrel with the notion that stories are one of our chief teaching tools. They might quarrel with the notion that play is the other and that mere lecturing runs a distant third. I also don't think that many would quarrel with the notion that stories have achieved far greater artistic heights than games have, despite the fact that <u>play probably *predates* story</u> (after all, even animals play, whereas stories require some form of language).

Are stories superior? We often speak of <u>wanting to make a game that makes players cry.</u> The classic example is the text adventure game *Planetfall*, where Floyd the robot sacrifices himself for you. But it happens outside of player control, so it isn't a challenge to overcome. It's grafted on, not part of the game. What does it say about games that the <u>peak emotional moment usually cited actually involves *cheating*</u>?

Games do better at <u>emotions that relate to mastery.</u> Stories can get these too, however. Getting emotional effects out of games may be the wrong approach—perhaps a better question is whether stories can be fun in the way games can.

Stories are a powerful teaching tool in their own right, but games are not stories.

When we speak of enjoyment, we actually mean a constellation of different feelings. Having a nice dinner out can be fun. Riding a roller coaster can be fun. Trying on new clothes can be fun. Winning at table tennis can be fun. Watching your hated high school rival trip and fall in a puddle of mud can be fun. Lumping all of these under "fun" is a rather horribly vague use of the term.

Different people have classified this differently. Game designer Marc LeBlanc has defined eight types of fun: sense-pleasure, make-believe, drama, obstacle, social framework, discovery, self-discovery and expression, and surrender. Paul Ekman, a researcher on emotions and facial expressions, has identified literally dozens of different emotions—it's interesting to see how many of them only exist in one language but not in others. Nicole Lazzaro did some studies watching people play games, and she arrived at four clusters of emotion represented by the facial expressions of the players: hard fun, easy fun, altered states, and the people factor.

My personal breakdown would look a lot like Lazzaro's:

- **Fun** is the act of mastering a problem mentally.

- **Aesthetic appreciation** isn't always fun, but it's certainly enjoyable.

- **Visceral reactions** are generally physical in nature and relate to physical mastery of a problem.

- **Social status maneuvers** of various sorts are intrinsic to our self-image and our standing in a community.

All of these things make us feel good when we're successful at them, but lumping them all together as "fun" just renders the word meaningless. So throughout this book, when I have referred to "fun," I've meant only the first one: mentally mastering problems. Often, the problems mastered are aesthetic, physical, or social, so fun can appear in any of those settings. That's because all of these are feedback mechanisms the brain gives us for successfully exercising survival tactics.

Of course, learning patterns is
not the only thing that is entertaining.
Humans enjoy primate dominance games,
for example. You could argue that
jockeying for status is also a challenge,
of course.

Physical challenges alone aren't fun. The feeling of triumph when you break a personal record is. Endurance running can be immensely satisfying but you have not solved a puzzle. It is not the same high as when you win a well-fought game of soccer thanks to your teamwork.

Similarly, autonomic responses aren't fun in and of themselves. You have them developed already, so the brain only rewards you for doing them in the context of a mental challenge. You don't get a high from just typing, you get it from typing while pondering what to say, or from typing during a typing game.

Social interactions of all sorts are often enjoyable as well. The constant maneuvering for social status that all humans engage in is a <u>cognitive exercise</u> and therefore essentially a game. There is a constellation of positive emotions surrounding interpersonal interactions. Almost all of them are signals of either pushing someone else down, or pushing yourself up, on the social ladder. Some of the most notable include:

social interactions

- **Schadenfreude**, the gloating feeling you get when a rival fails at something. This is, in essence, a put down.

- **Fiero**, the expression of triumph when you have achieved a significant task (pumping your fist, for example). This is a signal to others that you are valuable.

- **Naches**, the feeling you get when someone you mentor succeeds. This is a clear feedback mechanism for tribal continuance.

- **Kvell**, the emotion you feel when bragging about someone you mentor. This is also a signal that you are valuable.

- **Grooming behaviors**, a signal of intimacy often representing relative social status.

- **Feeding other people**, which is a very important social signal in human societies.

A lot of these feel good, but they aren't necessarily "fun."

We also enjoy visceral experiences of various sorts—
these are often challenges to ourselves.

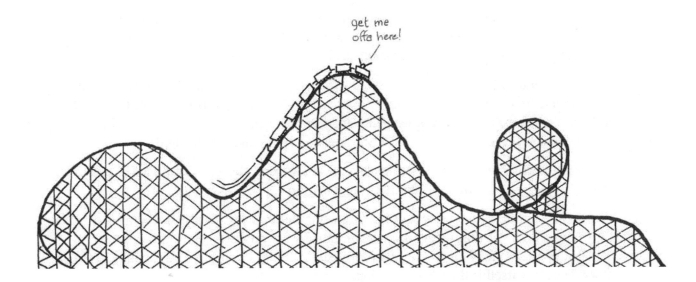

Aesthetic appreciation is the most interesting form of enjoyment. Science fiction writers call it "sensawunda." It's awe, it's mystery, it's harmony. I call it delight. Aesthetic appreciation, like fun, is about patterns. The difference is that aesthetics is about *recognizing* patterns, not learning new ones.

Delight strikes when we recognize patterns but are surprised by them. It's the moment at the end of *Planet of the Apes* when we see the Statue of Liberty. It's the thrill at the end of the mystery novel when everything falls into place. It's looking at the Mona Lisa and seeing that smile hovering at the edge of known expressions and matching it to our hypothesis of what she's thinking. It's seeing a beautiful landscape and thinking all is right in the world.

Why does a beautiful landscape make us feel that way? Because it meets our expectations, and *exceeds* them. We find things beautiful when they are very close to our idealized image of what they should be but with an additional surprising wrinkle. A perfectly closed off plot, with just a couple of loose threads. A picture of a farmhouse, but the paint is peeling. Music that comes back to the tonic note and then drops a whole step further to end on an unresolved minor seventh. It sends us chasing off after new patterns.

Beauty is found in the tension between our expectation and the reality. It is *only* found in settings of extreme order. Nature is full of extremely ordered things. The flowerbed bursting its boundaries is expressing the order of growth, the order of how living things stretch beyond their boundaries, even as it is in tension with the order of the well-manicured walkway.

Delight, unfortunately, doesn't last. It's like the smile from a beautiful stranger in a stairwell—it's fleeting. It cannot be otherwise—recognition is not an extended process.

You can regain delight by staying away from the object that caused it previously, then returning. You'll get that recognition again. But it's not quite what I would call fun. It's something else—our brains rewarding us for having learned well. It is the epilogue to the story. The story itself is the fun of learning.

story, not extended

94

Last, people often take DELIGHT in things that are not challenges.

mastering

Fun, as I define it, is the feedback the brain gives us when we are absorbing patterns for learning purposes. Consider the basketball team that says, "We went out there to have fun tonight," versus the one that says, "We went out there to win." The latter team is approaching the game as no longer being practice. Fun is primarily about practicing and learning, not about exercising mastery. Exercising mastery will give us some other feeling, because we are doing it *for a reason,* such as status enhancement or survival.

mastery

The lesson here is that *fun is contextual.* The reasons why we are engaging in an activity matter a lot. School is not usually all that fun because we take it seriously—it's not practice, it's for real, and your grades and social standing and clothing determine whether you are in the in-crowd or whether you sit at the table close to the cafeteria kitchen.

It's very telling that when we lose a competition, we often say, "Well, I was just doing it for fun." The implication is that we are shrugging off the implicit loss of social status inherent in a loss. Since it was merely a form of practice, perhaps we didn't put forth our best effort.

We get positive feedback for climbing the social ladder. We're just tribal monkeys throwing feces at each other in order to own the top of the tree. But notice some of the subtleties there: climbing it while helping others (naches and kvell). Climbing it while pushing the boundaries of our knowledge (fun). Climbing it while strengthening our social networks, building communities and families that work together to improve everyone's lot (grooming, pairing, and feeding others).

As monkeys go, that's pretty darn good. In the general run of animals, it's amazing. It's a lot better than being a shark that only gets feedback for eating.

I think there's a good case to be made that having fun is a key evolutionary advantage right next to opposable thumbs in terms of importance. Without that little chemical twist in our brains that makes us enjoy learning new things, we might be more like the sharks and ants of the world.

96

But delight tends to wear thin very quickly.
Real fun comes from challenges that are always at the margin of our ability.

So how does it feel? Well, the moment a lot of players like to cite is "being in the zone." If you get academic about it, you might reference Csikszentmihalyi's concept of "flow." This is the state you enter when you are experiencing absolute concentration on a task. When you're in absolute control, the challenges that come at you are met precisely by your skills. Lazzaro called this "hard fun," and it's the state from which you are most likely to emerge feeling either frustration or triumph.

Flow doesn't happen very often, but when it does it feels pretty darn wonderful. The problem is that precisely matching challenges to capability is incredibly hard. For one thing, the brain is churning away and might make a cognitive leap at any moment, rendering the rest of the challenge trivial. For another, whatever is presenting the challenges doesn't necessarily have any sense of the level of understanding possessed by the player.

As we succeed in mastering patterns thrown at us, the brain gives us little jolts of pleasure. But if the flow of new patterns slows, then we won't get the jolts and we'll start to feel boredom. If the flow of new patterns increases beyond our ability to resolve them, we won't get the jolts either because we're not making progress.

When there's flow, players usually say afterward, "That was a *lot* of fun." When there isn't flow, they might say "that was fun" somewhat less emphatically. The absence of flow doesn't preclude fun—it just means that instead of a steady drip-drip-drip of endorphins, you're getting occasional bits. And in fact, there can be flow that isn't fun—meditation induces similar brain waves, for example.

So fun isn't flow. You can find flow in countless activities, but they aren't all fun. Most of the cases where we typically cite flow relate to exercising mastery, not learning.

To recap the preceding pages: Games aren't stories. Games aren't about beauty or delight. Games aren't about jockeying for social status. They stand, in their own right, as something incredibly valuable. Fun is about learning in a context where there is no pressure, and that is why games matter.

When the balance is really perfect, people often zone out.

CHAPTER SIX: DIFFERENT FUN FOR DIFFERENT FOLKS

We all know that people learn at different rates and in different ways. Research has shown that people's learning patterns are with them at birth. Some people visualize things when they think of them; others are more verbal. Some people employ logic readily; others rely on leaps of intuition. We're all familiar with the bell curve distribution of IQ— and we're also familiar with the fact that IQ tests do not measure all forms of intelligence. Howard Gardner said there were in fact seven forms:

1. Linguistic

2. Logical-mathematical

3. Bodily-kinesthetic

4. Spatial

5. Musical

6. Interpersonal

7. Intrapersonal (internally directed, self-motivated)

There aren't really standardized tests for these other types of intelligences. Certainly, the list suggests right off the bat that these different people will be interested in different sorts of games because of their natural talents. Keep in mind that people are not likely to tackle patterns and puzzles that appear as noise to them; they'll likely select problems that they think they have a chance at solving. Hence the folks with bodily-kinesthetic intelligence will gravitate toward sports, whereas the linguistic folks may end up with crossword puzzles or *Scrabble*.

Not everyone is the same, of course.
Some people have musical talent,
others can integrate equations in their heads,
and others are intensely charismatic.

In recent years, much study has been centered on gender differences. It has finally become acceptable to discuss this topic without accusations of sexism. It's important to realize that in all cases, we're speaking in generalities, of averages. On average, females tend to have greater trouble with certain types of spatial perception—for example, visualizing the cross section of an arbitrary shape that has been rotated to a different facing. Conversely, males tend to have greater trouble with language skills—doctors have long known that it takes longer for boys to become verbally proficient.

It speaks well of the power of video games that they can actually change this. After all, the equation is both nature *and* nurture. Research has shown that if women who have trouble with spatial rotation tests are given a video game that encourages them to practice rotating objects and matching particular configurations in 3-D, not only will they master the spatial perception necessary, but the results will be *permanent.*

One researcher in the U.K., Simon Baron-Cohen, has concluded that there are "systematizing brains" and "empathizing brains." He identifies extreme systematizing brains as being autistic and ones just slightly less so as being those diagnosed as having Asperger's syndrome. The distribution curve of systematizing brains versus empathizing brains, according to Baron-Cohen, is apparently influenced by gender. Men are more likely to have systematizing brains, and women more likely to have empathizing brains.

According to Baron-Cohen's theory, there are people who have high abilities in both systematizing and empathizing. One would surmise that these people tend to go into the arts, which are heavily systematic and also require a high degree of empathy. Baron-Cohen postulates that having high abilities in both is a contraindicated survival trait since it means that they are almost certainly not as good at either as the "specialists." This may explain all those consumptive poets dying in garrets.

But as we tell our kids,
if you work hard enough,
you can overcome deficiencies.
Talent is no substitute for hard work.

Another way to look at this is not in terms of intelligence but in terms of learning styles. Here again, gender shows itself. Men not only navigate space differently, but they tend to learn by trying, whereas women prefer to learn through modeling another's behavior.

The classic ways of looking at learning styles and personalities are the Keirsey Temperament Sorter and the Myers-Briggs personality type. These are the ones with the four letter codes like INTP, ENFJ, and so on. Of course, there's also astrology, enneagrams, and lots of others. We can debate the validity of the various methods, but it does seem clear that they sort people into categories based on *something* and that there are different sorts of people in the world.

It's clear that players tend to prefer certain types of games in ways that seem to correspond to their personalities.

It is equally clear that different people bring different experiences to the table that leave them with differing levels of ability in solving given types of problems. Even things that are more fundamental than that may change over time; for example, the levels of hormones such as estrogen and testosterone fluctuate pretty significantly over the course of a life, and it's been shown that these affect personality.

What does this all mean for game designers? It means that not only will a given game be unlikely to appeal to everyone, but that it is probably impossible for it to do so. The difficulty ramp is almost certain to be wrong for many people, and the basic premises are likely to be uninteresting or too difficult for large segments of the population.

Since different brains
have different strengths
and weaknesses,
different people
will have different
ideal
games.

This may indicate a fundamental problem with games. Since they are formal abstract systems, they are by their very nature biased toward certain types of brains, just as books are biased. (Most book purchases in the U.S. are made by women, and half are made by individuals over the age of 45.)

For years now, the video game industry has struggled with the lack of appeal of games to the female audience. Many reasons have been advanced for this—the rampant sexism in video games, the lack of a retail channel that reaches the female demographic, the juvenile themes, the fact that there are relatively few female creators in the industry, the fact that the games focus on violence.

Perhaps the answer is simpler. Maybe games are more likely to appeal to young males because these players happen to have the sort of brain that works well with formal abstract systems. If so, you'd expect to see the following:

- Female players would gravitate toward games with simpler abstract systems and less spatial reasoning and more emphasis on interpersonal relationships, narrative, and empathy. They would also prefer games with simpler spatial topologies.

- There would be clear gender differences in play style between hardcore gamers of different genders. Males would focus on games emphasizing the projection of power and the control of territory, whereas females would select games that permit modeling behavior (such as multiplayer games) and do not demand strict hierarchies.

- As males aged, you'd expect them to slowly shift over to play styles similar to those of the women. Many of them might outright drop out of the gaming hobby. In contrast, older females likely wouldn't drop out of gaming—if anything, their interest in them might actually sharpen after menopause.

- There would be fewer female gamers in general since no matter what, games are still about formal abstract systems at heart.

People will usually choose to play the games they are already good at, that reflect their strengths.

As it happens, we *do* see all of these in demographic data of game players (along with much more). Games may be doomed to be the province of 14-year-old boys because that's what games select for.

As games become more prevalent in society, however, we'll likely see more young girls using the amazing brain-rewiring abilities of games to train themselves up—in other words, doubling down and reaching high levels of achievement on both sides of the fence. Recently, research was announced showing that girls who play "boys' games" such as sports tend to break out of traditional gender roles years later, whereas girls who stick to "girls' games" tend to adhere to the traditional stereotypes more strictly.

This argues pretty strongly that if people are to achieve their maximum potential, they need to do the hard work of playing the games they *don't* get, the games that *don't* appeal to their natures. Taking these on may serve as the nurture part of the equation, counterbalancing the brains that they were born with. The result would be people who move freely between worldviews, who bring a wider array of skills to bear on a given problem.

The converse trick, of training boys up, is harder for games to achieve because it does not play to the strength of games as a medium. Nonetheless, games should try. The thought that games are limited because of their fundamentally mathematical nature is somewhat depressing; it hasn't stopped music from being a highly emotional medium, and language manages to convey mathematical thoughts, so there is hope for games yet.

Arguably, they should seek out the games that address their weaknesses instead.

THEATRE TWO
HEARTS in LOVE →

2+2=4

Cheating

CHAPTER SEVEN: THE PROBLEM WITH LEARNING

Learning can be problematic. For one thing, it's kind of hard work. Our brains may unconsciously direct us to learn, but if we're pushed by parents, teachers, or even our own logical brains, we often resist most mightily.

When I was a kid taking math classes, teachers always made us write out proofs. We were good enough at algebra where we could look at a given problem and see the answer and then write it down, but it didn't matter—we had to actually work it out:

$x^2 + 5 = 30$

We weren't allowed to just write x = 5. We had to write out:

$\therefore x^2 = 30 - 5$

$\therefore x^2 = 25$

$\therefore x = \sqrt{25}$

$\therefore x = 5$

We always thought this was stupid. If we could just look at the problem and see that x = 5, why the hell couldn't we just write it down? Why go through the pesky process? All it did was slow us down!

Of course, the good reason is that multiplying -5 by -5 is also 25, and thus there are actually two answers. Skipping to the end, we're more likely to forget that.

That doesn't stop <u>the human mind from wanting to take shortcuts</u> however.

Since games are teaching tools,
players seeking to advance in a game
will always try to optimize what they are doing.

* "Kind sir, have you any unorthodox, mayhap quasi-legal, approaches to the game of chess?" (h.f. deadspeak)

Once a player looks at a game and ascertains the pattern and the ultimate goal, they'll try to find the optimal path to getting there. And one of the classic problems with games of all sorts is that players often have little compunction about violating the theoretical "magic circle" that encompasses games and makes them protected spaces in which to practice.

In other words, many players are willing to cheat.

This is a natural impulse. It's not a sign of people being bad (though we can call it bad sportsmanship). It's actually a sign of lateral thinking, which is a very important and valuable mental skill to learn. When someone cheats at a game, they may be acting unethical, but they're also exercising a skill that makes them more likely to survive. It's often called "cunning."

Cheating is a long-standing tradition in warfare, where it is acknowledged as one of the most powerful and brilliant of all military techniques. "Let's throw sand in our opponent's eyes." "Let's attack by night." "Let's not charge out of the woods and ambush them instead." "Let's make them walk through the mud so we can shoot them full of arrows." As one of the most important strategic adages has it, "If you cannot choose the battle, at least choose the battlefield."

When a player cheats in a game, they are choosing a battlefield that is broader in context than the game itself.

Cheating is a sign that the player is in fact grokking the game. From a strict evolutionary point of view, cheating is a winning strategy. Duelists who shoot first while their opponent is still pacing off are far more likely to reproduce.

If they are clever
and see an optimal path—

an Alexandrine solution
to a Gordian problem—

they'll do that instead of the
"intended gameplay."

There's a good reason why we instinctively and jealously preserve the notions of sportsmanship and fair play. If the lesson taught by a particular game comes up in the real world, the cheat may not work. Cheating may not prepare us correctly. This is why kicking an opponent during a soccer match is considered poor form. Whatever soccer's underlying mechanics are teaching us, kicking an opponent is outside its formal framework.

Players and designers often make the distinction between "cheating" and "exploiting a loophole." They always struggle to define this, but it boils down to whether or not the extraneous action is one that resides within the *magic circle of the game's framework* or not. Unsurprisingly, exploiters are often the *most* expert players of a game. They see the places where the rules don't quite jibe. This is also why they often think that it's unfair when sticklers for the rules tell them that what they did is not allowed. Their logic goes something like "if the game permits it, then it's legal."

But the game is usually intended to put players through a particular challenge, and while a bad design may allow the player to circumvent the challenge, we resent it *because* it's circumvention. It's not exactly evidence of mastery of a technique to solve the problem. Often games are trying to teach techniques, they don't merely give players goals and tell them to solve them any way they please.

We can rectify this to a degree via good game design (and even better, we can make games that don't prescribe solutions—that's a rather limited game, and it severely undermines what games are about). But in the end, we're fighting a losing battle against a natural human tendency: to get better at things.

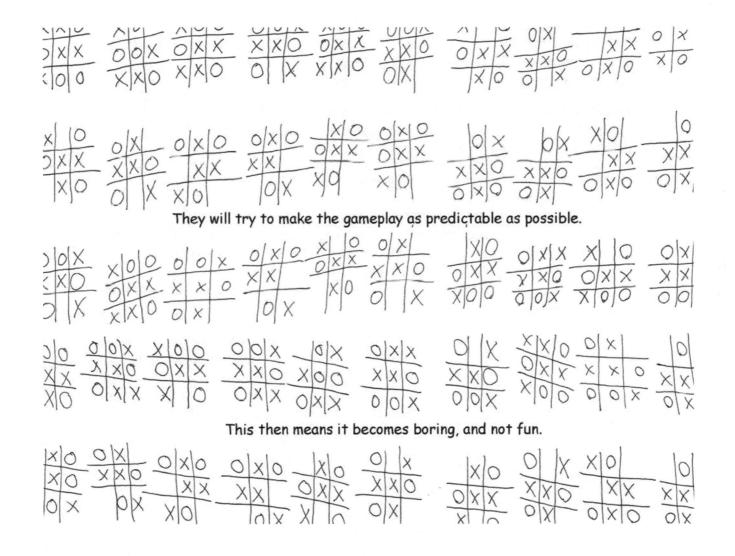

They will try to make the gameplay as predictable as possible.

This then means it becomes boring, and not fun.

115

Consider the oddity of games that intentionally create situations that we have long since moved past in the real world: games about fighting wars with bayonets, games about sailing ships, or games about an artisan-based economy. We've advanced in technology, and we have cruise missiles, aircraft carriers, and factories now.

Games, however, do not permit progress. Games do not permit innovation. They present a pattern. Innovating out of a pattern is by definition outside the magic circle. You don't get to change the physics of a game.

Human beings are *all* about progress. We like life to be easier. We're lazy that way. We like to find ways to avoid work. We like to find ways to keep from doing something over and over. We dislike tedium, sure, but the fact is that we crave *predictability*. Our whole life is built on it. Unpredictable things are stuff like drive-by shootings, lightning bolts that fry us, smallpox, food poisoning—unpredictable things can *kill* us! We tend to avoid them. We instead prefer sensible shoes, pasteurized milk, vaccines, lightning rods, and laws. These things aren't perfect, but they do significantly reduce the odds of unpredictable things happening to us.

And since we dislike tedium, we'll allow unpredictability, but only inside the confines of predictable boxes, like games or TV shows. Unpredictability means new patterns to learn, therefore unpredictability is fun. So we like it, for enjoyment (and therefore, for learning). But the stakes are too high for us to want that sort of unpredictability under normal circumstances. That's what games are for in the first place—to package up the unpredictable and the learning experience into a space and time where there is no risk.

The natural instinct of a game player is to make the game more predictable because then they are more likely to win.

In the real world, we call this "security" and "steady jobs" and "sensible shoes" and "routine."

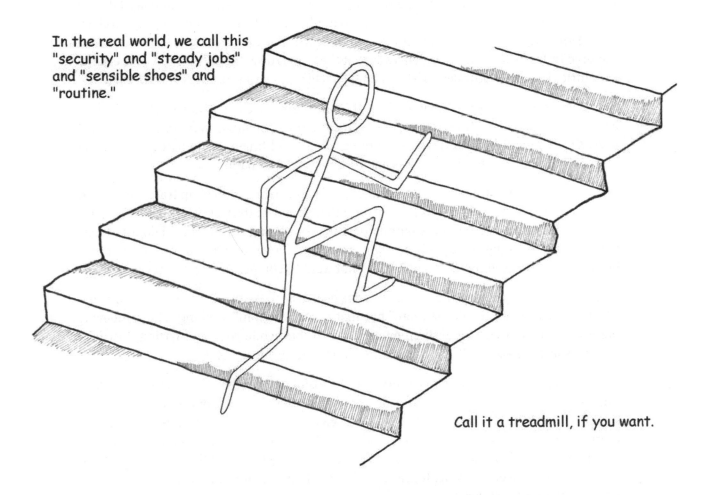

Call it a treadmill, if you want.

designers evolve responses

This leads to behaviors like "bottom-feeding," where a player will intentionally take on weaker opponents under the sensible logic that a bunch of sure wins is a better strategy than gambling it all on an iffy winner-take-all battle. Players running an easy level two hundred times to build up enough lives so that they can cruise through the rest of the game with little risk is the equivalent of stockpiling food for winter: it's just *the smart thing to do*.

This is what games are *for*. They teach us things so that we can minimize risk and know what choices to make. Phrased another way, *the destiny of games is to become boring, not to be fun*. Those of us who want games to be fun are fighting a losing battle against the human brain because fun is a process and routine is its destination.

glitches are fun

So players often intentionally suck the fun out of a game in hopes they <u>can learn something new</u> (in other words, find something fun) once they complete the task. They'll do it because they perceive it (correctly) as the optimal strategy for getting ahead. They'll do it because they see others doing it, and it's outright unnatural for a human being to see another human being succeeding at something and not want to compete.

All of this happens because the human mind is <u>goal driven</u>. We make pious statements like "it's the journey, not the destination," but that's mostly wishful thinking. The rainbow is pretty and all, and we may well enjoy gazing at it, but while you were gazing, lost in a reverie, someone else went and dug up the pot of gold at the end of it.

<u>Reward</u>s are one of the key components of a successful game activity; if there isn't a quantifiable advantage to doing something, the brain will often discard it out of hand. What are the other fundamental components of a game element, the atoms of games, so to speak? Game designer Ben Cousins calls these "ludemes," <u>the basic units of gameplay</u>. We've talked about several of them, such as "visit everywhere" and "get to the other side." There are many left to discover, we hope. In the end, though, they are almost always made up of the same elementary particles.

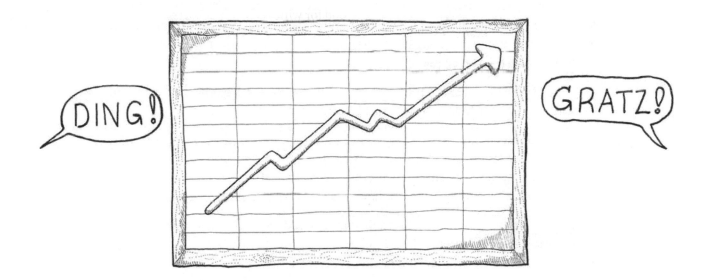

Game makers are fighting a losing battle against the human brain,
which always fights to optimize, assembly-line, simplify, maximize ROI.

Successful games tend to incorporate the following elements:

- **Preparation.** Before taking on a given challenge, the player gets to make some choices that affect their odds of success. This might be healing up before a battle, handicapping the opponent, or practicing in advance. You might set up a strategic landscape, such as building a particular hand of cards in a card game. Prior moves in a game are automatically part of the preparation stage because all games consist of multiple challenges in sequence.

- **A sense of space.** The space might be the landscape of a war game, a chess board, the network of relationships between the players during the bridge game.

- **A solid core mechanic.** This is a puzzle to solve, an intrinsically interesting rule set into which content can be poured. An example might be "moving a piece in chess." The core mechanic is usually a fairly small rule; the intricacies of games come from either having a lot of mechanics or having a few, very elegantly chosen ones.

- **A range of challenges.** This is basically content. It does not *change* the rules, it operates *within* the rules and brings slightly different parameters to the table. Each enemy you might encounter in a game is one of these.

- **A range of abilities required to solve the encounter.** If all you have is a hammer and you can only do one thing with it, then the game is going to be dull. This is a test that tic-tac-toe fails but that checkers meets; in a game of checkers you start learning the importance of forcing the other player into a disadvantageous jump. Most games unfold abilities over time, until at a high levels you have many possible stratagems to choose from.

- **Skill required in using the abilities.** Bad choices lead to failure in the encounter. This skill can be of any sort, really: resource management during the encounter, failures in timing, failures in physical dexterity, and failures to monitor all the variables that are in motion.

120

In fact, most gamers are so bottom-line that if an activity doesn't give a quantifiable reward, they'll consider it irrelevant.

A game having all of these elements hits the right cognitive buttons to be fun. If a game involves no preparation, we say it relies on chance. If there's no sense of space, we call it trivial. If there's no core mechanic, there's no game at all. If there's no range of challenges, we exhaust it quickly. If there's no multiple choices to make, it's simplistic. And if skill isn't required, it's tedious.

There are also some features that should be present to make the experience a learning experience:

- **A variable feedback system.** The result of the encounter should not be completely predictable. Ideally, greater skill in completing the challenge should lead to better rewards. In a game like chess, the variable feedback is your opponent's response to your move.

- **The Mastery Problem must be dealt with.** High-level players can't get big benefits from easy encounters or they will bottom-feed. Inexpert players will be unable to get the most out of the game.

- **Failure must have a cost.** At the very least there is an opportunity cost, and there may be more. Next time you attempt the challenge, you are assumed to come into it from scratch—there are no—"do-overs." Next time you try, you may be prepared differently.

Looking at these elementary particles that make up ludemes, it's easy to see why most games in history have been competitive head-to-head activities. It's the easiest way to constantly provide a new flow of challenges and content.

Most long lasting games in the past
<u>have been competitive</u>
because they lead to an endless supply
<u>of similar yet slightly varied puzzles.</u>

as each seek to exploit the other

123

Historically, competitive game-playing of all sorts has tended to squeeze out the people who *most* need to learn the skills it provides, simply because they aren't up to the competition and they are eliminated in their first match. This is the essence of the Mastery Problem. Because of this, a lot of people prefer games that take no skill. These people are definitely failing to exercise their brains correctly. *Not requiring skill from a player should be considered a cardinal sin in game design.* At the same time, designers of games need to be careful not to make the game demand too much skill. They must keep in mind that players are always trying to reduce the difficulty of a task. The easiest way to do that is to not play.

This isn't an algorithm for fun, but it's a useful tool for checking for the *absence* of fun because designers can identify systems that fail to meet all the criteria. It may also prove useful in terms of game critique. Simply check each system against this list:

- Do you have to prepare before taking on the challenge?

- Can you prepare in different ways and still succeed?

- Does the environment in which the challenge takes place affect the challenge?

- Are there solid rules defined for the challenge you undertake?

- Can the rule set support multiple types of challenges?

- Can the player bring multiple abilities to bear on the challenge?

- At high levels of difficulty, does the player *have* to bring multiple abilities to bear on the challenge?

- Is there skill involved in using an ability? (If not, is this a fundamental "move" in the game, like moving one checker piece?)

- Are there multiple success states to overcoming the challenge? (In other words, success should not have a single guaranteed result.)

Of course, if your opponent isn't an even match, the puzzle will be too easy or too hard.

- Do advanced players get no benefit from tackling easy challenges?

- Does failing at the challenge at the very least make you have to try again?

If your answer to any of the above questions is "no," then the game system is probably worth readdressing.

Game designers are caught in the Red Queen's Race because challenges are meant to be surmounted. The result is that modern game designers have often taken the approach of piling more and more different types of challenges into one game. The number of ludemes reaches astronomical proportions. Consider that checkers consists of exactly two: "capture all the pieces" and "move one piece." Now compare that to the last console game you saw.

Most classic games consist of relatively few systems that fit together elegantly. The entire genre of abstract strategy games is about elegant choice of ludemes. But in today's world, many of the lessons we might want to teach might require highly complex environments and many moving parts—online virtual worlds spring to mind as an obvious example.

The lesson for designers is simple: A game is destined to become boring, automated, cheated, and exploited. Your sole responsibility is to know what the game is about and to ensure that the game teaches that thing. That one thing, the theme, the core, the heart of the game, might require many systems or it might require few. But *no system should be in the game that does not contribute toward that lesson*. It is the cynosure of all the systems; it is the moral of the story; it is the point.

In the end, that is both the glory of learning and its fundamental problem: Once you learn something, it's over. You don't get to learn it again.

In fact, the desperate hunt for more puzzles to put into a given game has led to something called "kitchen-sink design."

IT'S A MASSIVELY MULTIPLAYER STRATEGY-BASED REAL-TIME SHOOTER WITH RPG CHARACTER DEVELOPMENT, PUZZLE GAME COMBAT, A RACING SUBGAME, AND YOU PLAY IT ON A DANCE MAT!

...please, I want this job to end...

NEW!

E3 EXCLUSIVE!

POWERED BY 55VIDEO CARDS

LEVEL UP!

CHAPTER EIGHT: THE PROBLEM WITH PEOPLE

The holy grail of game design is to make a game where the challenges are never ending, the skills required are varied, and the difficulty curve is perfect and adjusts itself to exactly our skill level. Someone did this already, though, and it's not always fun. It's called "life." Maybe you've played it.

That hasn't stopped us from trying all sorts of tactics to make games self-refreshing. You see, designing rule sets and making all the content is hard. Designers often feel proudest of designing good abstract systems that have deep self-generating challenges—games like chess and go and *Othello* and so on.

- **"Emergent behavior"** is a common buzzword. The goal is new patterns that emerge spontaneously out of the rules, allowing the player to do things that the designer did not foresee. (Players do things designers don't expect *all the time,* but we don't like to talk about it.) Emergence has proven a tough nut to crack in games; it usually makes games easier, often by generating loopholes and exploits.

- **We also hear a lot about storytelling.** It's easier to construct a story with multiple possible interpretations than it is to construct a game with the same characteristics. However, most games melded with stories tend to be Frankenstein monsters. Players tend to either skip the story or skip the game.

- **Placing players head-to-head** is also a common tactic, on the grounds that other players are an endless source of new content. This is accurate, but the Mastery Problem rears its ugly head. Players hate to lose. If you fail to match them up with an opponent who is very precisely of their skill level, they'll quit.

- **Using players to generate content** is a useful tactic. Many games expect players to supply the challenges in various ways, ranging from making maps for a shooter game to contributing characters in a role-playing game.

But is this futile? I mean, all these designers are trying to expand the possibility space…

Game designers talk a lot about emergent gameplay, non-linear storytelling, and player-entered content— they're all ways of increasing the possibility space, making self-refreshing puzzles.

(insert cartoon here.)

...and all the players are trying to reduce it, just as fast as they can. You see, humans are wired in some interesting ways. If something has worked for us before, we'll tend to do it again. We're really very resistant to learning. We're conservative at heart, and we grow more so as we age. You've perhaps heard the old saw, variously attributed to Clemenceau, Churchill, and Bismarck, "If a man isn't liberal when he's 20, he has no heart. If he's not conservative when he's 40, he has no brain." Well, there's a lot of truth to this. We grow more resistant to change as we age, and we grow less willing (and able) to learn.

If we come across a problem we have encountered in the past, our first approach is to try the solution that has worked before, even if the circumstances aren't exactly the same.

The problem with people isn't that they work to undermine games and make them boring. That's the natural course of events. The real problem with people is that

...even though our brains feed us drugs to keep us learning...

...even though from earliest childhood we are trained to learn through play...

...even though our brains send incredibly clear feedback that we should learn throughout our lives...

PEOPLE ARE LAZY.

The interesting thing is that people
tend to come to a given puzzle and
try to apply known solutions.

Look at the games that offer the absolute greatest freedom possible within the scope of a game setting. In role-playing games there are few rules. The emphasis is on collaborative storytelling. You can construct your character any way you want, use any background, and take on any challenge you like.

And yet, people choose the *same* characters to play, over and over. I've got a friend who has played the big burly silent type in literally dozens of games over the decade I have known him. Never once has he been a vivacious small girl.

Different games appeal to different personality types, and not just because particular problems appeal to certain brain types. It's also because particular *solutions* appeal to particular brain types, and when we've got a good thing going, we're not likely to change it. This is not a recipe for long-term success in a world that is constantly changing around us. Adaptability is key to survival.

Much is made of cross-gender role-play in online settings. When you look at it in this light, it's clearly because a given gender presentation is a *solution choice*—a tool the player is using to solve problems presented by the online setting. It might be because the gender presentation is a good way to meet like-minded people. Males choosing female avatars may be signaling something about their preference for the company of other empathizing brains, for example.

Sticking to one solution is not a survival trait anymore. The world is changing very fast, and we interact with more kinds of people than ever before. The real value now lies in a wide range of experiences and in understanding a wide range of points of view. Closed-mindedness is actively dangerous to society because it leads to misapprehension. And misapprehension leads to misunderstanding, which leads to offense, which leads to violence.

Consider the hypothetical case where every player of an online role-playing game gets exactly two characters: one male and one female. Would the world be more or less sexist as a result?

For example, players of online role-playing games tend to play
the same character types in game after game after game.

THE ONLINE RPG RORSCHACH TEST

Another case where the wiring of the human brain tends to betray us lies in the seductive feeling of make-believe mastery.

Engaging in an activity that you have fully mastered, being in the zone, feeling the flow, can be a heady experience. And no one can deny the positive effects of meditation. That said, the point at which a player chooses to repeatedly play a game they have already mastered completely, just because they like to feel powerful, is the point at which the game is betraying its own purpose. Games need to encourage you to *move on*. They are not there to fulfill power fantasies.

Ah, but is it seductive! Because games exist within the confines of "let's pretend," they also offer a lack of consequences. They are libertine in their freedoms. They let you be a godlet. To the person that perhaps does not get enough sense of control in their real lives, the game may offer something rather…persuasive.

Making you feel good about yourself in a pretend arena isn't what games are for. Games are for offering challenges, so that you can then turn around and apply those techniques to real problems. Going back through defeated challenges in order to pass time isn't a productive exercise of your brain's abilities. Nonetheless, lots of people do it.

Some choose to play for "style points," which is at least a sign that they are creating new challenges for themselves. But once you get past the point of doing something perfectly, do yourself a favor and *quit the game*.

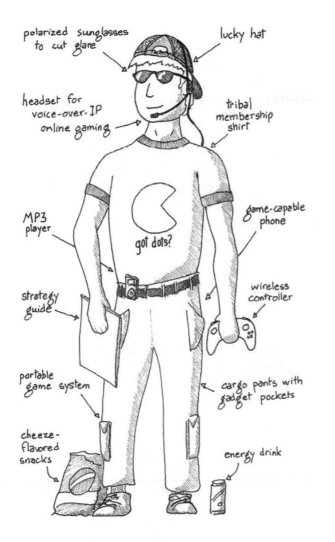

polarized sunglasses to cut glare

lucky hat

headset for voice-over-IP online gaming

tribal membership shirt

got dots?

MP3 player

game-capable phone

strategy guide

wireless controller

portable game system

cargo pants with gadget pockets

cheeze-flavored snacks

energy drink

HOMO POWERLUDENS

Found in a variety of habitats. Typically makes their nest in couches, chairs, and sometimes arcade cabinets. Believed to have evolved from *h. pinballwizardicus*. Generally harmless, and breeds easily in captivity.

And if gamers find themselves
in tune with a game,
they may play it far
longer than they need
to in order to master it,
because being in the zone feels good.

There are other sorts of audience problems with games. One of them has proven fatal to many genres of games: the problem of increasing complexity. Most art forms have swung in pendulum fashion from an Apollonian to a Dionysian style—meaning, they have alternated between periods where they were reserved and formal and where they were exuberant and communicative. From Romanesque to Gothic churches, from art rock to punk, from the French Academy to Impressionism, pretty much every medium has had these swings.

Games, however, are always formal. The historical trend in games has shown that when a new genre of game is invented, it follows a trajectory where increasing complexity is added to it, until eventually the games on the market are so complex and advanced that newcomers can't get into them—the barrier of entry is too high. You could call this the jargon factor because it is common to *all* formal systems. Priesthoods develop, terms enter common usage, and soon only the educated few can hack it.

In most media, the way out of this has been the development of a new formal principle (as well as a cultural shift). Sometimes it was a development in knowledge of the form. Sometimes it was the development of a competing medium that usurped the place of the old medium, as when photography forced painters to undergo a radical reevaluation of their art form. Games, though, aren't tending to do this all that much. By and large, we have seen an inexorable march toward greater complexity. This has led to a priesthood of those who can speak the language, master the intricacies, and keep up-to-date.

Every once in a while games come along that appeal to the masses, and thank goodness. Because frankly, priesthoods are a perversion of what games are about as well. The worst possible fate for games (and by extension, for our species) would be for games to become niche, something played by only a few elite who have the training to do so. It was bad for sports, it was bad for music, it was bad for writing, and it would be bad for games as well.

Conversely, it's possible that instead games are like the Twonky from the famous science fiction story. Maybe the kids will keep up, and the older people won't be able to. And then we'll get left behind…

Some gamers will have broad experience with games, and that lets them see a given game and quickly grok the entire pattern.

They end up flitting from game to game like butterflies.

All of these are cases where human nature works against the success of games as a medium and as a teaching tool. Ironically, these all converge most sharply in the most unlikely of candidates, the person who loves games more than anyone: the game designer.

Game designers spend less time playing individual games than the typical player does. Game designers finish games less often than typical players do. They have less time to play a given game because they typically sample so many of them. And perniciously, they are just as likely, if not more so because of business pressures, to turn to known solutions.

Basically, game designers suffer from what I call "designeritis." They are hypersensitive to patterns in games. They grok them very readily and move on. They see past fiction very easily. They build up encyclopedic recollections of games past and present, and they then theoretically use these to make new games.

But they usually *don't* make new games because their very experience, their very library of assumptions, holds them back. Remember what the brain is doing with these chunks it builds—it is trying to create a generically applicable library of solutions. The more solutions you have stored up, the less likely you are to go chasing after a new one.

The result has been, as you would expect, a lot of derivative work. Yes, you need to know the rules in order to break them, but given the lack of codification and critique of what games are, game designers have instead operated under the more guildlike model of apprenticeship. They do what they have seen work.

The most creative and fertile game designers working today tend to be the ones who make a point of *not* focusing too much on other games for inspiration. Creativity comes from cross-pollination, not the reiteration of the same ideas. By making gaming their hobby, game designers are making an echo chamber of their own work. Because of this, it is critical that games be placed in context with the rest of human endeavor so that game designers can feel comfortable venturing outside their field in search of innovative ideas.

DESIGNERITIS

YOU BOUGHT **HOW** MANY GAMES?

...30?

AND YOU'RE **DONE** WITH THEM ALL?

UMM... YES?

AFTER **HOW** LONG?

UH... TEN MINUTES EACH?

...it's better return than a chocolate bar, right?

Game designers
often play a given game
for only fifteen minutes or so.

It can be hard to play
for enjoyment rather than
for analysis.

CHAPTER NINE: GAMES IN CONTEXT

Game designers are doing something that really isn't their job—they are evolving game design into a discipline. And it's a good thing that they are doing it. This has been happening slowly over the past few decades and particularly in the past 10 years.

mature medium

I don't necessarily mean they are becoming all scientific about it. But we have seen the following: a large increase in the number of books about game design, the beginnings of a critical vocabulary, and the creation of academic programs that attempt to engage in critique. In short, the field has started to move away from the hit-and-miss shots-in-the-dark approach and toward an understanding of what games are and how they work. This is an important final step in the maturation process of a medium.

On the facing pages where you usually see what are hopefully amusing cartoons, I've filled out a few grids with different human endeavors. Bear with me—there are two sorts of people in this world, those who divide everyone into two sorts of people and those who don't.

Any given activity can be performed either by yourself or with others. If you are doing it with others, you can be working either with or against each other. I call these three approaches *collaborative, competitive,* and *solo.*

Down the side of our grid, I've made a subtler distinction. Are you a passive consumer of this activity? An audience member? Or do you actively work on the activity? If you are someone who doesn't work on the activity but instead lets the work of others wash over you, we'll call you interested in the *experiential* side of the activity—you want the experience.

Are you actually *creating* the experience? Then you are engaging in a *constructive* activity. Maybe instead, you are taking the experience apart, to see how it works. I used to label this destructive, but it's not really; often the original is left behind, intact though somewhat bruised and battered. So perhaps *deconstructive* is a better term.

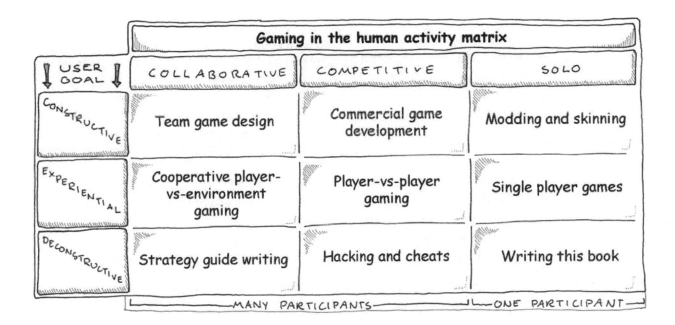

Gaming in the human activity matrix

↓ USER GOAL ↓	COLLABORATIVE	COMPETITIVE	SOLO
CONSTRUCTIVE	Team game design	Commercial game development	Modding and skinning
EXPERIENTIAL	Cooperative player-vs-environment gaming	Player-vs-player gaming	Single player games
DECONSTRUCTIVE	Strategy guide writing	Hacking and cheats	Writing this book
	←———— MANY PARTICIPANTS ————→		←— ONE PARTICIPANT —→

Of course, analyzing a game is just
another way of playing it, of pinning down the pattern in it.

My second grid shows how we can analyze music. When I look at the chart for music, what I see is a constellation of music-based entertainment. If I made a similar chart for books, it would cover prose-based entertainment. Basically, this chart can be applied to any *medium*.

"Game" is not a medium, even though I have misused it that way on almost every page of this book. It is, depending on the definition, one *use* of a medium. The medium is really an unwieldy phrase like "formal abstract models for teaching patterns." And once you see that, you see that even though fire drills or CIA model war games of the future of the Middle East may not necessarily be fun, they still belong on the chart. The fact that they are not fun has more to do with their implementation than with their intrinsic nature.

Interaction is possible in all media. Interacting with stage-based media is termed "acting" and interacting with prose-based media is termed "writing." There's been a lot of discussion in professional video game design circles lately about "the surrender of authorship" inherent in adding greater flexibility to games and in the burgeoning "mod" community. I think the key insight here is that players are simply "interacting with the medium."

In other words, modding is just playing the game in another way, sort of like a budding writer might rework plots of characters from other writers into derivative journeyman fiction or into fan fiction. The fact that some forms of it are constructive (modding a game), experiential (playing a game), or deconstructive (hacking a game) are immaterial; the same activities are possible with a given play, book, or song. Arguably, the act of literary analysis is much the same as the act of hacking a game—the act of disassembling the components of a given piece of work in a medium to see how it works, or even to get it to do things, carry messages, or otherwise represent itself as something other than what the author of the piece intended.

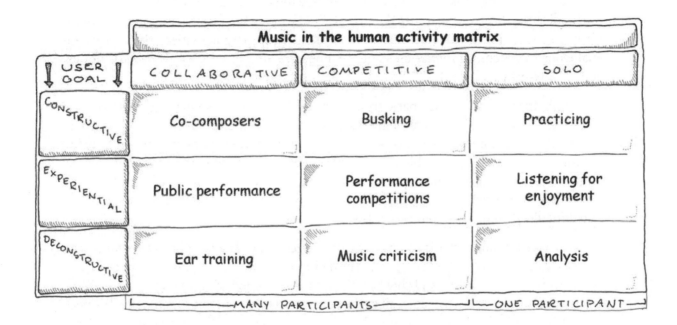

Music in the human activity matrix

USER GOAL ↓	COLLABORATIVE	COMPETITIVE	SOLO
CONSTRUCTIVE	Co-composers	Busking	Practicing
EXPERIENTIAL	Public performance	Performance competitions	Listening for enjoyment
DECONSTRUCTIVE	Ear training	Music criticism	Analysis

←————— MANY PARTICIPANTS —————→		←— ONE PARTICIPANT —→

This is no different from any other medium, really, or any other field of human endeavor.

Some of the activities on the first chart aren't what you would normally term "fun," even though they are almost all activities in which you learn patterns. We can sit here and debate whether performing music, writing a story, or drawing a picture is fun. From having training in all three, I can tell you that they are all hard work, which isn't something we necessarily consider fun. But I derive great fulfillment from these activities. This is perhaps analogous to watching *Hamlet* on stage, reading *Lord Jim,* or viewing *Guernica*—not exactly giggly-happy-fun, but fulfilling in a different way.

The chills that go down your back are not always indicative of something that you find enjoyable. A tragedy or moment of great sorrow can cause them. The moment you recognize a pattern your body will give you the chill as a sign. Just as writing isn't necessarily fun but might be something valuable for the writer to do, or practicing piano for hours on end might not be fun but something that gives fulfillment, engaging in interaction with games need not be fun either but might indeed be fulfilling, thought-provoking, challenging, and also difficult, painful, and even compulsive.

In other words, games can take forms we don't recognize. They might not be limited to being "a game" or even a "software toy." The definition of "game" implies certain things, as do the words "toy," "sport," and "hobby." The classic definition of "game" covers only some of the boxes in the grid. Arguably, all of the boxes in the grid are fun to *someone*. We need to start thinking of games a little more broadly. Otherwise, we will be missing out on large chunks of their potential as a medium.

The reason why the rise of critique and academia surrounding games is important is because it finally adds the missing element to put games in context with the rest of human endeavor. It means their arrival as a medium. Considering how long they have been around, they're a little late to the party.

144

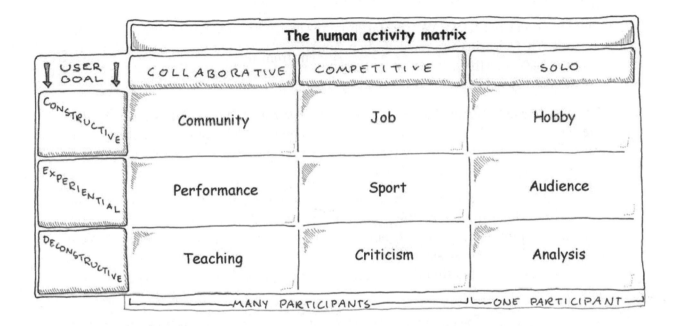

The human activity matrix

USER GOAL	COLLABORATIVE	COMPETITIVE	SOLO
CONSTRUCTIVE	Community	Job	Hobby
EXPERIENTIAL	Performance	Sport	Audience
DECONSTRUCTIVE	Teaching	Criticism	Analysis

MANY PARTICIPANTS — ONE PARTICIPANT

This suggests that critiquing games is not only valid,
but something praiseworthy.

It's important that we figure out how to do it correctly.

Once games are seen as a medium, we can start worrying about whether they are a medium that permits art. All other media do, after all.

Pinning art down is tricky. We can start from the basics, though. What is art for? Communicating. That's intrinsic to the definition. And (if you've bought into the premises of this book) we have seen that the basic intent of games is rather communicative as well—it is the creation of a symbolic logic set that conveys meaning.

Some apologists for games like to tout the fact that games are interactive as a sign that they are special. Others like to say that interactivity is precisely why games cannot be art, because art relies on authorial intent and control. Both positions are balderdash. Every medium is interactive—just go look on the grid.

So what is art? My take on it is simple. Media provide information. Entertainment provides comforting, simplistic information. And art provides challenging information, stuff that you have to think about in order to absorb. That's it. Art uses a particular medium to communicate within the constraints of that medium, and often what is communicated is thoughts *about* the medium itself (in other words, a formalist approach to arts—much modern art falls in this category).

The medium shapes the nature of the message, of course, but the message can be representational, impressionistic, narrative, emotional, intellectual, or whatever else. Some art forms are solo, and some are collaborative (and they can all be made collaborative to an extent, I believe). And some media are actually the result of the collaboration of specialists in many different media working together to present a work that is incomplete without the use of multiple media within it. Film is one such medium. And games are another.

To be or not
to be...

We often discuss the desire for games to be art—
for them to be puzzles with more than one right answer,
puzzles that lend themselves to interpretation.

One of the commonest points I hear about why video games are not an art form is that they are just for fun. They are just entertainment. Hopefully I've made it clear why that is a dangerous underestimation of fun. But most music is also just entertainment, and most novels are read just for fun, and most movies are mere escapism, and yes, even most pretty pictures are just pretty pictures. The fact that most games are merely entertainment does not mean that this is all they are doomed to be.

Mere entertainment becomes art when the communicative element in the work is either novel or exceptionally well done. It really is that simple. The work has the power to alter how people perceive the world around them. And it's hard to imagine a medium more powerful in that regard than video games, where you are presented with interactivity and a virtual world that reacts to your choices.

"Well done" and "novel" mean, basically, craft. You can have well-crafted entertainment that fails to reach the level of art. The upper reaches of art are usually subtler achievements. They are pieces of work that you can return to again and again and keep learning something new. The analogy for a game would be one you can replay over and over again and keep discovering new things.

Since games are closed formal systems, that might mean that games can never be art in that sense. But I don't think so. I think that means that we just need to decide what we want to say with a given game—something big, something complex, something open to interpretation, something where there is no single right answer—and then make sure that when the player interacts with it, they can come to it again and reveal whole new aspects to the challenge presented.

That may be the best definition of when something ceases to be craft and turns into art—

*drawing by Elena, age 7.

What would a game like this be?

It would be thought-provoking.

It would be revelatory.

It might contribute to the betterment of society.

It would force us to reexamine assumptions.

It would give us different experiences each time we tried it.

It would allow each of us to approach it in our own ways.

It would forgive misinterpretation—in fact, it might even encourage it.

It would not dictate.

It would immerse, and impose a worldview.

Some might say that abstract formal systems cannot achieve this. But I have seen wind course across the sky, bearing leaves; I have seen paintings by Mondrian made of nothing but colored squares; I have heard Bach played on a harpsichord; I have traced the rhythms of a sonnet; I have trod in the steps of a dance. All media are abstract, formal systems. Let's not sell abstraction and formality short.

—the point at which it becomes subject to interpretation.

In fact, the toughest puzzles are the ones that force the most self-examination. They are the ones that challenge us most deeply on many levels—mental stamina, mental agility, creativity, perseverance, physical endurance, and emotional self-abnegation. They come precisely from the interactive portions of the chart, when you look at other media.

Consider the act of creation.

It's one of the toughest things to do and do well, in human endeavor. And yet it is also one of our most instinctive actions; from a young age, we not only trace patterns but attempt to create new ones. We scribble with crayons, we ba-ba-ba our way through songs.

The fact that playing games—good ones, anyway—is fundamentally a creative act is something that speaks very well for the medium. Games, at their best, are not prescriptive. They demand that the user create a response given the tools at hand. It is a lot easier to fail to respond to a painting than to fail to respond to a game.

No other artistic medium defines itself around an intended *effect* on the user, such as "fun." They all embrace a wider array of emotional impact. Now, we may be running into definitional questions for the word "fun" here, obviously, but even so, I'd prefer to approach things from a more formalist perspective to actually arrive at what the basic building blocks of the medium are. From a formalist point of view, music can be considered ordered sound and silence, and poetry can be considered the placement of words and gaps between words, and so on.

The closer we get to understanding the basic building blocks of games, the things that players and creators alike manipulate in interacting with the medium, the more likely we are to achieve the heights of art.

There are many puzzles like this in life. Try writing a book.

It was a dark and stormy night.

Some folks disagree with me pretty vehemently on this. They feel that the art of the game lies in the formal construction of systems. The more artfully constructed the system is, the closer the game is to art.

Putting games in context with other media demands that we consider this viewpoint. In literature, it's called a *belles-lettristic* point of view. The beauty of poetry lies solely in the sound and not in the sense, according to those who feel this way.

And yet, even the shape of the sound can be put in context. Let's digress and consider some other media…

Impressionism is not concerned with giving impressions, but rather with a more distanced form of seeing, of mimesis. Modern image processing tools describe the Impressionist formal process (and indeed many of the later processes such as posterization) as *filters*—an accurate description in that Impressionist paintings are depictions not of an object or a scene, but of the play of light upon said object or scene. In such representations, you still must conform to all previously established rules of composition—color weight, balance, vanishing point, center of gravity, eye center, and so on—while essentially avoiding painting the object or scene itself, which ends up being absent from the finished work.

Impressionist music was based primarily on repetition; its influence on later minimalist styles is clear. However, where minimalism also restricts its harmonic vocabulary, often to just a few essential chords (tonic, dominant, subdominant, perhaps a few extensions or substitutions thereof), Impressionist music is essentially that of Debussy: intensely varied in orchestration, extremely complex, particularly in its chromatic harmonies, and nonetheless very repetitive melodically. Ravel's work as an orchestrator is perhaps the epitome of the Impressionistic style: his "Bolero" consists of the same passage played over and over, identical harmonically and melodically; it has merely been orchestrated differently at each repetition, and the dynamics are different. The sense of crescendo throughout the piece is achieved precisely though this repetition.

Id Est

R. Koster

Or composing music.

And of course, there was "Impressionist" writing. Virginia Woolf, Gertrude Stein, and many other writers worked with the idea that characters are unknowable. Books like *Jacob's Room* and *The Autobiography of Alice B. Toklas* play with the established notions of self and work toward a realization that other people are essentially unknowable. However, they also propose an alternate notion of knowability: that of "negative space," whereby a form is understood and its nature grasped by observing the perturbations around it. The term is from the world of pictorial art, which provides many useful insights when discussing the problem of mimesis.

All of these are organized around the same principles; that of negative space, that of embellishing the space around a central theme, of observing perturbations and reflections. There was a zeitgeist, it is true, but there was also conscious borrowing from art form to art form, and it occurs in large part because no art form stands alone; they bleed into one another.

Can you make an Impressionist game? A game where the formal system conveys the following?

- The object you seek to understand is not visible or depicted.

- Negative space is more important than shape.

- Repetition with variation is central to understanding.

The answer is, of course you can. It's called *Minesweeper*.

Or understanding your significant other.

In the end, the endeavor that games engage in is not at all dissimilar to the endeavors of any other art form. The principal difference is not the fact that they consist of formal systems. Look at the following lists:

- Meter, rhyme, spondee, slant rhyme, onomatopoeia, caesura, iamb, trochee, pentameter, rondel, sonnet, verse

- Phoneme, sentence, accent, fricative, word, clause, object, subject, punctuation, case, pluperfect, tense

- Meter, fermata, key, note, tempo, coloratura, orchestration, arrangement, scale, mode

- Color, line, weight, balance, compound, multiply, additive, refraction, closure, model, still life, perspective

- Rule, level, score, opponent, boss, life, power-up, pick-up, bonus round, icon, unit, counter, board

Let's not kid ourselves—the sonnet is caged about with as many formal systems as a game is.

If anything, the great irony about games, put in context with other media, is that they may afford less scope to the designer, who has less freedom to impose, less freedom to propagandize. Games are not good at conveying specifics, only generalities. It is easy to make a game that tells you that small groups can prevail over large ones, or the converse. And that may be a valuable and deeply personal statement to make. It's a lot harder to make a game that conveys the specific struggle of a group of World War II soldiers to rescue one other man from behind enemy lines, as the film *Saving Private Ryan* does. The designer who wants to use game design as an expressive medium must be like the painter and the musician and the writer, in that they must learn what the strengths of the medium are, and what messages are best conveyed by it.

Or designing games.

CHAPTER TEN: THE ETHICS
OF ENTERTAINMENT

Nobody actually interacts with games on an abstract level exclusively. You don't play the abstract diagrams of games that I have drawn on the facing pages; you play the ones that have little spaceships and laser bolts and things that go Boom. The core of gameplay may be about the emotion I am terming "fun," the emotion that is about learning puzzles and mastering responses to situations, but this doesn't mean that the other sorts of things we lump under fun do not contribute to the overall experience.

People like playing go using well-burnished beads on a wooden board and they like buying *Lord of the Rings* chess sets and glass Chinese checkers sets. The aesthetic experience of playing these games matters. When you pick up a well-carved wooden game piece, you respond to it in terms of aesthetic appreciation—one of the other forms of enjoyment. When you play table tennis against an opponent, you feel visceral sensations as you stretch your arm to the limit and smash the ball against the table surface. And last, when you slap the back of your teammate, congratulating him on his field goal, you're participating in the subtle social dance that marks the constant human exercise of social status.

We know this about other media. It matters who sings a song because delivery is important. We treasure nice editions of books, rather than cheap ones, even though the semantic content is identical. Rock climbing a real rock face, versus a fake one attached to a wall, feels different.

In many media, the presentation factors are outside the hands of the initial creator of the content. But in other media, the creator has a say. Often, we have a specific person whose role it is to create the overall experience as opposed to the content itself. And rightfully, this person is given higher authority over the final output than the content creator alone. The director trumps the writer in a movie, and the conductor trumps the composer in a symphony.

There is a difference between designing the content and designing the end-user *experience*.

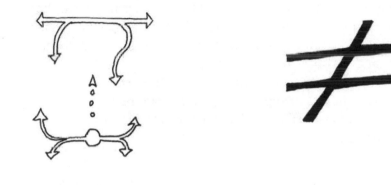 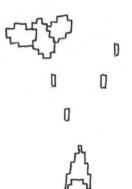

But designing games isn't just about the mechanics.

In most cases, we haven't reached this realization in game design. Game design teams are not set up this way. Nonetheless, it's an inevitable development in the medium. Too many other components have tremendous importance in our overall experience of games for their overall shape to rest in the hands of the designer of formal abstract systems alone.

Players see through the fiction to the underlying mechanics, but that does not mean the fiction is unimportant. Consider films, where the goal is typically for the many conventions, tricks, and mind-shapings that the camera performs to remain invisible and unperceived by the viewer. It's rare that a film tries to call attention to the gymnastics of the camera, and when it does, it will likely be to make some specific point. There are many techniques used by the director and the cinematographer, such as framing the shot of a conversation from slightly over the shoulder of the interlocutor to create a sense of psychological proximity, that are used transparently, without the viewer noticing, because they are part of the vocabulary of cinema.

For better or worse, visual representation and metaphor are part of the vocabulary of games. When we describe a game, we almost never do so in terms of the formal abstract system alone—we describe it in terms of the overall experience.

The dressing is tremendously important. It's very likely that chess would not have its long-term appeal if the pieces all represented different kinds of snot.

Even if players can see through fiction, the art of the game includes that fiction.

When we compare games to other art forms that rely on multiple disciplines for effect, we find that there are a lot of similarities. Take dance, for example. The "content creator" in dance is called the choreographer (it used to be called the "dancing master," but modern dance disliked the old ballet terms and changed it). Choreography is a recognized discipline. For many centuries, it struggled, in fact, because there was no notation system for dance. That meant that much of the history of this art form is lost to us because there was simply no way to replicate a dance save by passing it on from master to student.

And yet, the choreographer is not the ultimate arbiter in a dance. There are far too many other variables. There's a reason, for example, why the prima ballerina is such an important figure. The dancer makes the dance, just as the actor makes the lines. A poor delivery means that the experience is ruined—in fact, if the delivery is poor enough, the *sense* may be ruined, just as bad handwriting obscures the meaning of a word.

Swan Lake staged on the shore of a lake is a different experience from *Swan Lake* on a bare stage. There's a recognized profession there too—the set designer. And there's the lighting, the casting, the costuming, the performance of the music..The choreographer may be the person who creates the dance, but in the end, there's probably a director who creates the *dance*.

Games are the same way. We could probably use new terminology for games. Often in large projects, we make the distinction between game system designers, content designers, the lead designer or creative director (a problematic term because it means something else in different disciplines, such as in graphic design), writers, level designers, world builders, and who knows what else. If we consider games to be solely the design of the formal abstract systems, then only the system designer is properly a game designer. If we come up with a new term for the formal core of games, comparable to "choreography," then we'd give this person a title derived from that term instead.

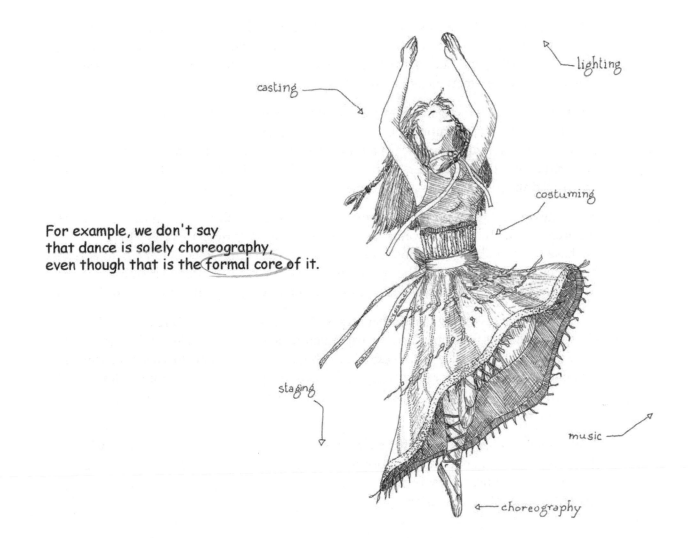

casting

lighting

costuming

For example, we don't say
that dance is solely choreography,
even though that is the formal core of it.

staging

music

choreography

All of this implies that a mismatch between the core of a game—the ludemes—and the dressing can result in serious problems for the user experience. It also means that the right choice of dressing and fictional theme can strongly reinforce the overall experience and make the learning experience more direct for players.

The bare mechanics of a game may indeed carry semantic freighting, but odds are that it will be fairly abstract. A game about aiming is a game about aiming, and there's no getting around that. It's hard to conceive of a game about aiming that isn't about shooting, but it has been done—there are several games where instead of shooting bullets with a gun, you are instead shooting pictures with a camera.

For games to really develop as a medium, they need to further develop the ludemes, not just the dressing. By and large, however, the industry has spent its time improving the dressing. We have better and better graphics, better back stories, better plots, better sound effects, better music, more fidelity in the environments, more types of content, and more systems within each game. But the systems themselves tend to see fairly little innovation.

It's not that progress along these other axes isn't merited—it's just *easy* relative to the true challenge, which is developing the formal structure of games themselves. Often these new developments improve the overall experience, but that's comparable to saying that the development of the 16-track recorder revolutionized songwriting. It didn't; it revolutionized arranging and production, but the demo versions of songs are still usually one person with a piano or a guitar.

The best test of a game's fun in the strict sense will therefore be playing the game with no graphics, no music, no sound, no story, no nothing. If that is fun, then everything else will serve to focus, refine, empower, and magnify. But all the dressing in the world can't change iceberg lettuce into roast turkey.

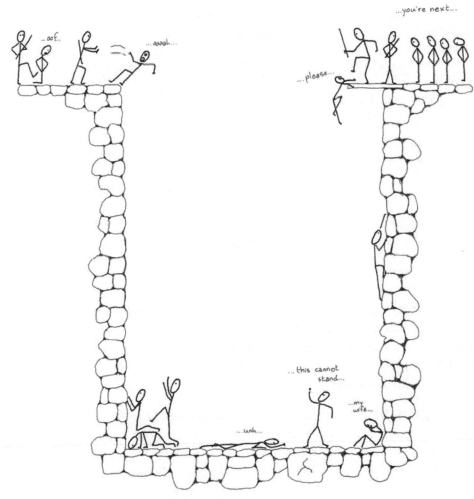

Consider a game of
mass murder where
you throw victims
down a well and they
stand on each other
to try to climb out.

This means the question of ethical responsibility rears its head. The ethical questions surrounding games as murder simulators, games as misogyny, games as undermining of traditional values, and so on are *not aimed at games themselves*. They are aimed at the *dressing*.

To the designer of formal abstract systems, these complaints are always going to seem misguided. A vector of force and a marker of territory have no cultural agenda. At the least, the complaints are misdirected—they *ought* to go to the equivalent of the director, the person who is making the call on the overall user experience.

Directing these complaints to the director is the standard. It's the standard to which we hold the writers of fiction, the makers of films, the directors of dances, and the painters of paintings. The cultural debate over the acceptable limits of content is a valid one. We all know that there is a difference in experience caused by presentation. If we consider the art of the dance to be the sum of choreography plus direction plus costuming and so on, then we must consider the art of the game to be the ludemes plus direction plus artwork and so on.

The bare mechanics of the game do not determine its semantic freight. Let's try a thought experiment. Let's picture a mass murder game wherein there is a gas chamber shaped like a well. You the player are dropping innocent victims down into the gas chamber, and they come in all shapes and sizes. There are old ones and young ones, fat ones and tall ones. As they fall to the bottom, they grab onto each other and try to form human pyramids to get to the top of the well. Should they manage to get out, the game is over and you lose. But if you pack them in tightly enough, the ones on the bottom succumb to the gas and die.

I do not want to play this game. Do you? Yet it is *Tetris*. You could have well-proven, stellar game design mechanics applied toward a quite repugnant premise. To those who say the art of the game is purely that of the mechanics, I say that film is not solely the art of cinematography or scriptwriting or directing or acting. The art of the game is the whole.

This does not mean that the art of the cinematographer (or ludemographer) is less; in truth, the very fact that the art of the film fails if *any* of its constituent arts fail elevates each and every one to primacy.

The mechanics may be Tetris,
but the experience is very different.

The danger is philistinism. If we continue to regard games as trivial entertainments, then we will regard games that transgress social norms as obscene. Our litmus test for obscenity centers on redeeming social value, after all. There is no doubt that the dressing of games may or may not have any redeeming social value. But it is important to understand that the ludemes themselves can have social value. By that standard, all good games should pass the litmus test regardless of their dressing.

Creators in all media have a social obligation to be responsible with their creations. Consider the recent development of "hate crime shooters," where the enemies represent an ethnic or religious group that the creators dislike. The game mechanic is old and tired and offers nothing new in this case. We can safely consider this game to be hate speech, as it was almost certainly intended.

The problematic case is a game that contains both brilliant gameplay and offensive content. The commonest defense is to argue that games do not exert significant influence on their players. This is untrue. *All* media exert influence on their audiences. But it is almost always the *core* of the medium that exerts the most influence because the rest is, well, dressing.

All artistic media have influence, and free will also has a say in what people say and do. Games right now seem to have a very narrow palette of expression. But let them grow. Society should not do something stupid like the Comics Code, which stunted the development of the comics medium severely for decades. Not all artists and critics agree that art has a social responsibility. If there was such agreement, there wouldn't be the debates about the ethics of locking up Ezra Pound, about the validity of propagandistic art, about whether one should respect artists who were scoundrels and scum in their private lives. It's not surprising that we wonder whether games or TV or movies have a social responsibility—once upon a time we asked the same thing about poetry. Nobody really ever agreed on an answer.

The constructive thing to do is to push the boundary gently so that it doesn't backfire. That's how we got *Lolita* and *Catcher in the Rye,* how we got *Apocalypse Now.* As a medium, we have to earn the right to be taken seriously.

The literal lesson being taught is still how to stack blocks, but the artistic statement is different.

CHAPTER ELEVEN: WHERE GAMES SHOULD GO

I've spent a lot of time talking about how games intersect the human condition. I think there is an important distinction to be drawn, however. In other media, we frequently speak of how a given work is revelatory of the human condition. By this, we mean that the work is a good portrayal of the human condition—it is something that gives us insight into ourselves. As the Greeks put it, *gnothi seauton*—know thyself. It's perhaps the greatest challenge we as humans face, and in many ways, it may be the greatest threat to our survival.

Many of the things that I have discussed in this book, such as theories of cognition, understanding of gender, learning styles, chaos theory, graph theory, and literary criticism, are fairly recent developments in human history. Humanity is engaged in a grand project of self-understanding, and most of the tools we have used in the past were imprecise at best. Over time we have developed better tools at a glacial pace in the quest to understand ourselves better.

It's an important endeavor because other humans have typically been our greatest predator. Today we have come to realize how interrelated we all are even though the left continent doesn't know what the right continent is doing. We have come to realize that actions we undertake often have far-reaching consequences that we never anticipated. Some, such as James Lovelock, have gone so far as to call us all one giant organism.

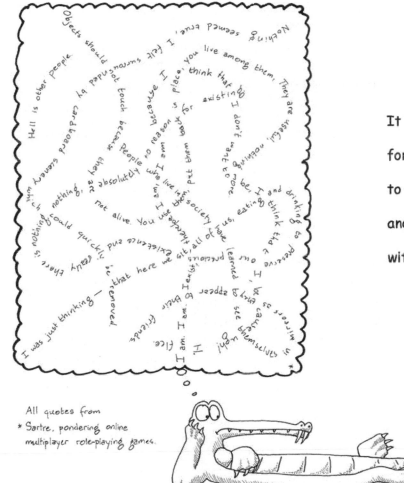

It is not the same thing

for our games

to portray the human condition

and the human condition to exist

within our games.

All quotes from
* Sartre, pondering online multiplayer role-playing games.

I'm not being all that fanciful or idealistic in saying that we are in many ways trembling on the threshold of a far deeper understanding of ourselves than ever before, thanks to advances as diverse as medical imaging, network theory, quantum physics, and even marketing. Given how much of our view of the world is shaped by our perceptions and the way we filter information as it reaches us, clarifying our understanding of that filter is bound to significantly reshape our relationship to the world.

In this light, it's interesting to see how many of the most famous quotes of Jean-Paul Sartre seem eerily applicable to our relationship to the virtual worlds created by games. Students of philosophy would tell you that he was simply recognizing the artificiality of every world we perceive, since they are all mental constructs in the end.

Games thus far have not really worked to extend our understanding of ourselves. Instead, games have primarily been an arena where human behavior—often in its crudest, most primitive form—is put on display.

There is a crucial difference between games portraying the human condition and the human condition merely existing within games. The latter is interesting in an academic sense, but it is unsurprising. The human condition manifests anywhere. We may come to better understanding of ourselves by examining our *relationship* to games, as this book attempts to do, but for games to truly step up to the plate, they need to provide us with insights into ourselves.

but if we play with instead of playing in

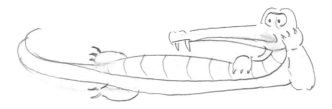

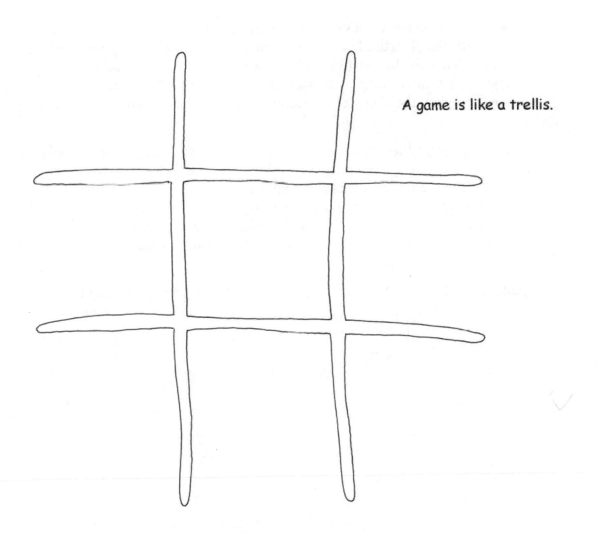

A game is like a trellis.

Right now, most games are about violence. They are about power. They are about control. This is not a fatal flaw. Practically any form of entertainment is about sex and violence, if you want to look at basic building blocks. It's just that they are contextualized into love, yearning, jealousy, pride, coming of age, patriotism, and other subtler concepts. If you took out all the sex and all the violence, you wouldn't have very many movies, books, or TV shows.

While we're bemoaning the lack of maturity in the field, we need not to miss the forest for the trees. Too much sex and violence isn't the problem. The problem is *shallow* sex and violence. This is why we decry casual player killing in an online world, why we snicker at puerile chat sex logs, why we resent seeing bouncing boobies in the beach volleyball game, and why we are disturbed by the portrayals of ethnicities and women. And also why we get excited to hear of the possibility for meaningful conflict in games or get defensive about the "reality" of online relationships.

We should fix the fact that the average cartoon does a better job at portraying the human condition than our games do.

what to do w IDENTITY + empathy !

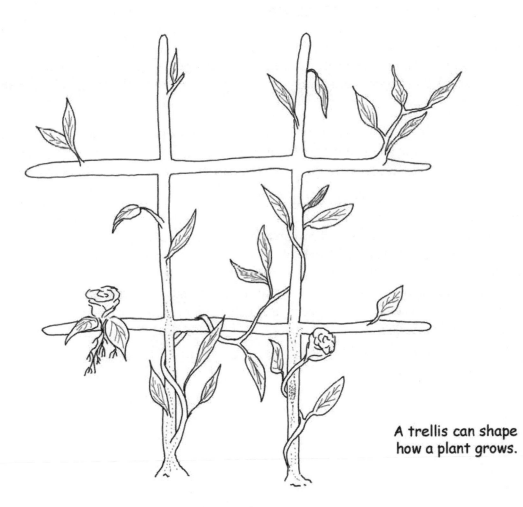

A trellis can shape
how a plant grows.

I have been using the analogy of a trellis. If people are the plants and the game is the trellis, it should not surprise us that the plants are shaped to some degree by the trellis. It also shouldn't surprise us that the plants grow to escape the trellis. Both of these are merely in the nature of the plant. It learns from its environment and its inborn nature both, and it works to escape those confines, to progress, to reproduce and be the tallest plant in the garden.

When we look at the great works of art, however, they are shaped in special ways. They are trellises that form the plant in particular directions. They have intent behind them, and they have the purpose of achieving something in particular with the growth of that plant.

Not all fields have discovered the knack to this. Storytelling mastered it long, long ago. Music discovered that something in the combination of certain frequencies of sound, certain rates of sound wave pulses, and certain combinations of timbres could be combined to achieve specific, targeted effects. Relatively recently, we have seen the field of architecture come to a realization that the shape of the space we walk in can be formed with intent—we can be made angry, inquisitive, friendly, or antisocial by means of how we divide spaces, how high we vault a ceiling, where we permit natural light, where people walk, and what colors we paint the walls.

179

The reason why games as a medium are not mature, despite their prehistoric origins, is not because we haven't reliably mastered creating fun, or do not have a vocabulary to define fun, or terminology to describe features or mechanics. It's not because we only know how to create power fantasies.

It's because when you feed a plant through a musical trellis, the trellis-maker can shape the plant to many possible forms. When you feed a plant through a literary trellis, the writer can shape the plant to many possible forms.

When you feed a player through a game trellis, right now, we know only "fun" and "boring." Mastery of the medium of games will have to imply authorial intent. The formal systems must be capable of invoking desired learning patterns.

If they can't, then games are a second-rate art form, and always will be.

examples

I am not going to pretend I know how to achieve this. But I see glimmers of hope in many games. I see the possibility of creating games where the rules are informed by our understanding of human beings themselves—counters that react according to the newly discovered rules of human minds.

We know how to create games where the formal mechanics are about climbing a ladder of status. I don't know how to make a game that is about the loneliness of being at the top, but I think I can see how we might get there.

For games to reach art,
the trellis itself,
the mechanics,
must be revelatory of
the human condition.

side grade! (vs. upgrade)

Consider a game in which you gained power to act based on how many people you *controlled* but you gained power to heal yourself from attacks based on how many *friends* you had. Then include a rule that friends tend to fall away as you gain power. This is expressible in mathematical terms. It fits within an abstract formal system. It is also an artistic statement, a choice made by the designer of the ludeme.

Now, the tough part—the game's victory condition must not be about being on top or being at the bottom. Instead, the goal must be something else—perhaps ensuring the overall survival of the tribe.

Now, suddenly, we see that being at the top, and having no allies, is a choice. Being lower in the status hierarchy is also a choice, and it may be a more satisfying choice. The game is presenting a pattern and a lesson with a specific desired outcome. We need the right feedback in place as well, of course: we should reward all players for sacrificing themselves for the good of the tribe. Perhaps if they are captured in the course of the game, they may no longer act directly but still score points based on the actions of the players they *used* to rule. This would represent their legacy—an important psychological driver that mere power fantasies tend not to tackle.

idea of subtlety

There are many possible lessons to be extracted from such a game, and there's no right answer to the question of choice of strategy. It is simply representing some aspects of the world as it is. It's crude, and not worked out in detail, but it is an example of a game that might actually teach something subtler than tactics in a simulated battle. We begin to create mechanics that simulate not the projection of power, but lofty concepts like duty, love, honor, and responsibility, and evolutionary ones like "I want my children to have a better life than mine."

The obstacles to making games—trellises—that shape plants in ways we choose are not mechanical ones. The obstacle is a state of mind. It's an attitude. It's a worldview.

Fundamentally, it is intent.

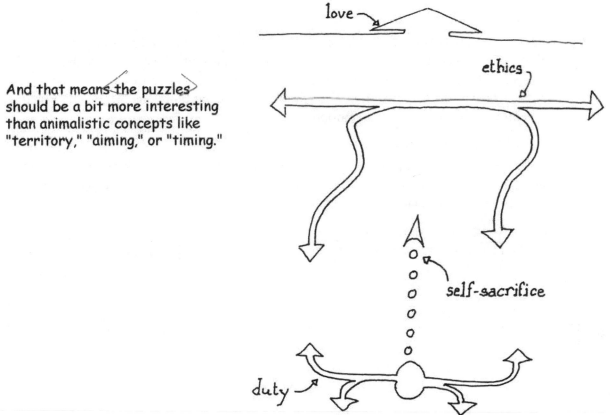

And that means the puzzles should be a bit more interesting than animalistic concepts like "territory," "aiming," or "timing."

CHAPTER TWELVE: Taking Their Rightful Place

There are games that accomplish this—the work of Dani Bunten Berry comes to mind. But far too many games do not do so with conscious intent. Games have the capability to sit on the shelf next to all other communications media. They are capable of art. They are capable of portraying the human condition. They are teaching tools. They carry socially redeeming content. They elicit emotion.

But we have to *believe* that they do, in order for them to reach their potential. We have to go into the systems design process, the ludeme-building process, aware that they have this potential and this capability. We have to consider ourselves as artists, as teachers, as people with a powerful tool that can be taken up.

It's time for games to move on from only teaching patterns about territory, aiming, timing, and the rest. These subjects aren't the preeminent challenges of our day.

do games need to address these challenges?

Games deserve to sit on the shelf right next to all other communications media, once the medium is mature.

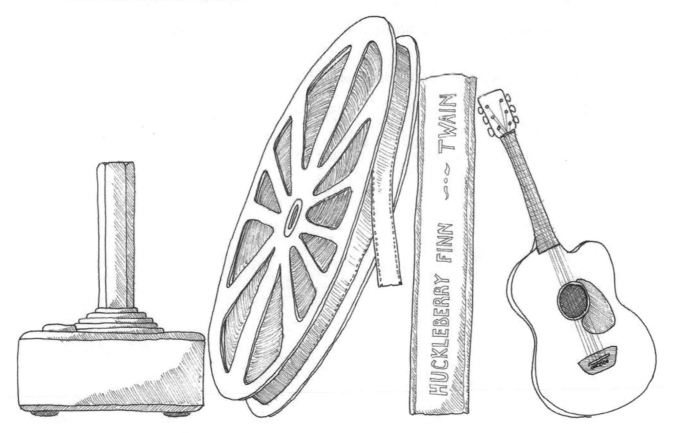

Games do not need to be able to evoke an unexpected tear, like the *Pietà*.

Games do not need to be able to rouse us to anger against injustice, like *Uncle Tom's Cabin*.

Games do not need to be able to send us spiraling into awe, like Mozart's *Requiem*.

Games do not need to leave us hovering at the boundary of understanding, like Duchamp's *Nude Descending a Staircase*.

Games do not need to record the history of our souls, like *Beowulf*.

They may not be able to, in fact. We would not necessarily ask architecture or dance to accomplish all of those things either.

But games *do* need to illuminate aspects of ourselves that we did not understand fully.

do they do this already?

The point at which our game puzzles
approach the complexity of the puzzles
in other art forms
is the point at which
the game art form

becomes mature.

=

but how can
starry night
be played?

Games do need to present us with problems and patterns that do not have one solution, because those are the problems that deepen our understanding of ourselves.

Games do need to be created with formal systems that have authorial intent.

Games do need to acknowledge their influence over our patterns of thought.

Games do need to wrestle with the issues of social responsibility.

Games do need to attempt to apply our understanding of human nature to the formal aspects of game design.

Games do need to develop a critical vocabulary so that understanding of our field can be shared.

Games do need to push at the boundaries.

The gap between those who want games to entertain
and those who want games to be art does not exist

2B || !(2B)

To be or
not to be...

Most importantly, games and their designers need to acknowledge that there is no distinction between art and entertainment. Viewed in context with human endeavor and what we know of how our inner core actually *works*, games are not to be denigrated. They are not trivial, childish things.

In no other medium do the practitioners assume that just because they're paying their dues, they cannot create something capable of changing the world. Nor should game designers.

All art and all entertainment are posing problems to the audience. All art and all entertainment are prodding us toward greater understanding of the chaotic patterns we see swirl around us. Art and entertainment are not terms of *type*—they are terms of *intensity*.

because all art entails posing questions and puzzles—
tough ones, ethical ones even.
And games will never be mature
as long as designers create them with
complete answers to their own puzzles in mind.

Why? Because people are lazy, yet people also want a better life for their children. That is the blind urge that drives all humanity, all life. A legacy is what motivates the selfish genes embedded in the warp and weft of our bodies.

so-called "bad fans"

Let's be frank with ourselves. We all know that most people, most of the audience out there, is complacent. They are very willing to settle for easy entertainment. They are more than up for another evening in the Barcalounger in front of a sitcom that teaches the same lessons that the one on last week did.

We call this "pop music." We call it "mass market." And games are indeed reaching for this mass market, and I suppose that to a degree I am fighting in the tide in arguing that that is not the ultimate destiny for games any more than it is for any other art form. The art we remember is material that opened up new vistas; whether or not it was popular at the time is largely an accident of history. Shakespeare was a popular playwright and then was forgotten for a couple hundred years. Popularity is not a measure of long-term evolutionary success.

Of course, we all know that most people are too comfortable to want to be challenged in that way.

another
gratuitous
penguin

art is more challenging now

A tremendous amount of the content pumped through media today has as its goal mere comforting, confirming, and cocooning. We gravitate toward the music we already like, the morals we already know, the characters who behave predictably.

Seen in the most pessimistic light, this is irresponsible. When the world shifts around those people, they will lack the tools to adapt. The calling of the creator is to provide those people with the tools to adapt, so that when the world changes and is swept along the currents of cultural change, those folks in the Barcaloungers are swept along with them and the march of human advancement continues.

There will always be a class of player who prefers the comfort of tackling only puzzles they know how to solve.

Play developed to teach us about survival. For many cultural reasons, we have allowed it to take a place in human culture where it is denigrated, minimized, and assumed to be worthless. And yet there's a cultural undercurrent that operates at the instinctive level, an undercurrent that mourns the ways in which play is removed from our lives.

Games mattered to us in prehistoric days. It may be that we've outgrown the simplistic lessons they were able to teach and that, when we reach adulthood, we do in fact put aside childish ways.

But my kids are showing me that childhood is also a state of mind. It is an ongoing quest for learning.

I, for one, don't want to put that aside, and I don't think anyone else should either.

In the caveman days, the wolves and tigers got 'em.

In the end, if I can say with a straight face after a day's work making games that one person out there learned to be a better leader, a better parent, a better co-worker; learned a new skill that kept them their job, a new skill that helped them advance the state of the art in their chosen field, a new skill that made their world grow a little…

Then I will know that my work was valuable. It was worthwhile. It was a contribution to society.

I'll be able to whisper to myself, "I do connect people."

"I do teach."

Hear that, grandpa?

I MAKE GAMES, AND IM PROUD OF IT.

do games teach relevent skills?

These days, we're a bit more tolerant—the job market gets them instead.

EPILOGUE: FUN MATTERS, GRANDPA

It's been a long journey for me, and I don't doubt that as my kids continue to grow, it will seem even longer.

I have watched them start to learn the concepts of respect for one another.

I have watched them understand that resources are limited and that things must be shared.

Every day, they connect an astounding number of new neurons; they learn a flabbergasting number of new words, and they develop in ways I can barely remember and barely glimpse.

Games are helping them along that path, and for that I am grateful. I'm not immune to the desire that my children be better off, after all, and I'll take any tool that helps us along that path.

A lot of old age is attributable to losing neurons, losing connections, losing the patterns we have built up, settling into fewer and fewer until all we can do is stand by helplessly as the world dissolves into noise around us. We'd all be better off if we kept our minds limber by pushing them to always tackle new problems.

Not too long before my grandfather died, he told me, "I'm thinking of getting one of those computer things. It doesn't seem like the Internet is all that different from ham radio. Maybe I'll give it a try."

Games are powerful tools for good—
they rewire people's brains, just like books and movies and music.

I learned of my grandfather's passing when I arrived at the hotel in San Jose, where I was attending the annual Game Developers Conference. Somehow it seems apropos.

The questions he posed, there in the wake of shootings at Columbine High School, there at a time when the world was suddenly making little sense, are fair questions.

Are games a tool for evil? Or for good? Are they frivolous at best or frivolous at worst?

It seems important that we know the answers, not just to allow those of us who work in this field to sleep better at night, but also in order to reassure those who watch us work: our families, our friends, our cultures.

202

People get scared of the
influence games have over them—
fears that they will cause murderous rampages on the streets. That's unlikely.

Games fit in the spectrum of human activity. Human activity is not always pretty. It's not always noble. It's not always altruistic. And a lot of really dumb things are done in games. A lot of dumb things are done by people playing games. A lot of dumb things are done by those making games.

But ignorance can be rectified. Human activity may be driven by selfish genes, by the phantasms of inaccurate perception, by reactionary tribalism and shortsighted dominance moves.

But there are those firemen, those special education teachers, those architects, who are out there working. They're building spaces in which we can live safely and rear our children.

I've put forth what may seem like a mechanistic view of the world in this book, one that would perhaps run contrary to my grandfather's deeply held religious faith. And yet I think that we would both come to the same conclusion:

Any striving for understanding that we do is likely to hold back the darkness. The new may scare us, as when symphonies with odd harmonies cause riots among disturbed music lovers...

But time smoothes things over. And we are left with beautiful music.

So my answer here is, I am willing to choose which side of human nature I want to foster.

Like story, and music, games and play
are fundamental parts of
how the human brain works,
and it's pretty rare for
symphonies to cause
riots...

FAMOUS CLASSICAL MUSIC RIOTS

1838

BERLIOZ
Benvenuto Cellini

1913

STRAVINSKY
Rite of Spring

1923

ANTHEIL
Ballet Mecanique

1917

SATIE
Parade

1926

RAVEL
Chansons Madecasses

I cannot blame my grandfather for being nervous about something that seemed very new, even though it was in fact very old. It is a natural reaction. It is the human reaction to the eruption of the unfamiliar.

Tracing the nature of fun, and the core of gameplay, has made me more comfortable in my own self with what I do, and why I do it.

We have a powerful tool here, one that is arguably underutilized even as it reaches new peaks of acceptance among people of all ages. We should take it up responsibly, with awareness of how it fits into culture, and with respect for its abilities.

The mere titling of a piece of music lends it narrative context and enriches it tremendously. Yes, it is possible to appreciate Penderecki's *Threnody for the Victims of Hiroshima* or any of the works of Aaron Copland without their titles, as pure sound. But the *sense* of them is carried in the interstices between the music and the title. Just as the *sense* of a film is carried in the webbing between the acting and the writing and the cinematography.

Other art forms have long recognized this; Welles's staging of *Macbeth* as a Haitian tale of vodoun, for example, achieved by selectively adjusting one of the component pieces of the art form.

All of which is by way of saying that I don't think we get to ignore the prostitutes, the sexism, the occasional racism, and the general crudity of the commercial game industry. The prostitute in *Grand Theft Auto* may be a power-up in mechanical terms. But in experiencing the game, it takes a game critic to divorce her from the context in which she appears. And frankly, game critique isn't even developed enough to give that particular game object and interaction a name.

My answer here is, I'm content with accepting my responsibility on that front.

This doesn't mean that game designers shouldn't act responsibly—

but then, all creators in all media should act responsibly.

If games are mere amusements, and my grandfather's concerns were valid, then by acting responsibly, and striving to make games that illuminate the human condition, I have at least caused no harm.

If I am going to noodle about with this medium simply because I think it's a nifty keen toy, the *least* I can do is make sure I don't hurt anyone else in the process. Even better, I can take this nifty keen toy very very very seriously and assume that it is a powerful tool for good or evil. And try to make it a tool for good.

It's Pascal's Wager. If it's all "just a game," I was just a crackpot all along. But if it's not.... There are only two responsible ways to behave with such a tool. Either step away from it altogether and let someone qualified take it up, or take it up and be as qualified as you can.

My reply is, I won't take a sucker bet.

do people get hurt? Do we care?

BLAISE PASCAL

IF GOD DOES NOT EXIST, IT DOESN'T MATTER IF I BELIEVE.

IF GOD DOES EXIST, THEN I HAD BETTER BE A BELIEVER.

IF I WERE A BETTING MAN, I'D SAY BELIEF IS THE SAFER BET!

If you think "it's just a game,"

consider Pascal's Wager.

The task I have to make my grandfather proud of what I do seems fairly simple, really. It's not that dissimilar to the role he took up each time he picked up his carpentry tools in his workshop.

Work hard on craft.

Measure twice, cut once.

Feel the grain; work with it, not against it.

Create something unexpected, but faithful to the source from which it sprang.

Strikes me as good advice for any act of creation. My reply is, I can do that.

The challenge game designers face is "how do we create games that do not have one right answer?"

My kids already play games and say things and do things that make me uncomfortable, just as I made games that made my grandfather uncomfortable. Some eggs need to be broken to make this omelet.

To achieve the potential of the medium, we're going to have to push at some boundaries and on some buttons that may make people rather uncomfortable. We'll assert that games are not only entertainment, and we will probably produce some work that may shock, or offend, or present themes that challenge deeply cherished beliefs.

That's not outlandish. All the other media do it.

My commitment is, I'll try to make sure that nobody gets hurt.

is this important?
what is "hurt"?

This may involve making games
with uncomfortable subject matter,

For all of us game designers, it means the extremely difficult task of reevaluating our roles in life. It means perceiving ourselves as having a responsibility to others, whereas we previously thought of ourselves as carefree. It means granting a greater level of respect to the tools we work with—the push and pull of mechanic and feedback, the intricate pathways of the human brain and human apprehension—and a greater level of respect to our audience.

They deserve more than just another jumping puzzle. We have to believe, as game designers, that we can deliver that, and we have to believe that we *should*.

To which I say, I believe.

do artists need to worry about this?
do scientists?

because having respect
for players implies
giving them real challenges,
challenges as sophisticated
as the best stories give them.

Last, it means that everyone else—the people like my grandfather—need to come to under-stand the valuable role we play in society. We're not geeks in the basement rolling funny-shaped dice. We're also the teachers of your children. We're not irresponsible 14-year-old boys (well, not all of us)—we're parents too. We're not splattering gore and sex on TV screens across the world merely for the sake of titillation.

Games deserve respect. We as creators must respect them, and do right by their potential. And the rest of the world must respect them and grant them the scope to become what they can and must.

So my answer is, yes, what we do is worthy of respect.

It also requires society to have respect for its own games.

It may be that even after everything I've said, everything all the other people working with games have said, society will continue to react in a knee-jerk fashion to the unfamiliar.

It may be that the current flowering of academic programs in game studies, and the fledging field of ludology, are an aberration and a frivolity.

But painting was once a blasphemous act that robbed reality of its essence. Dance was seen as wantonness incapable of expressing any higher emotions. The novel was self-indulgent gothic nonsense for cooped-up housewives. Film was once trashy kinetoscopes at the penny arcade, unworthy of adult attention. Jazz was devil music that would lead young lives astray. Rock h' roll was destroying the fabric of our country.

And Shakespeare himself was no more than a bit player and sometime scribbler for a theater in the bad part of town. Proper women weren't allowed because their reputations would be ruined, and their stepping on the stage was unthinkable.

We learned better.

It's still possible that this time we won't…

Someday, if society allows it, games will have their Shakespeare.

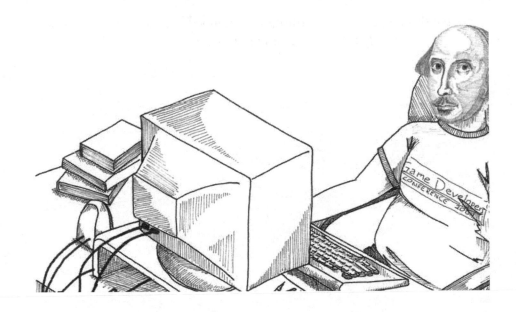

in which case we should pack up all the chess sets...

gather up the balls and the nets and the tops...

collect the dolls and the toy cars...

put them in that chest, the one at the top of the stairs...

the one we carry up to the attic...

to sit closed, hasp flipped but not locked, under the window...

We should put away the things of childhood and step into a world where the young, and the young at heart, are seen and not heard.

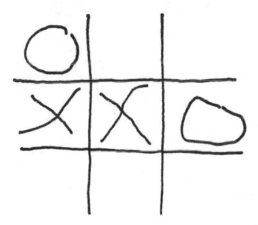

But if we fail to understand why games matter,
and how fun matters,
all our games are destined to be like tic-tac-toe.

To which I say,

No.

Because I'd hate to pass up that look of joy and wonder in my children's eyes.

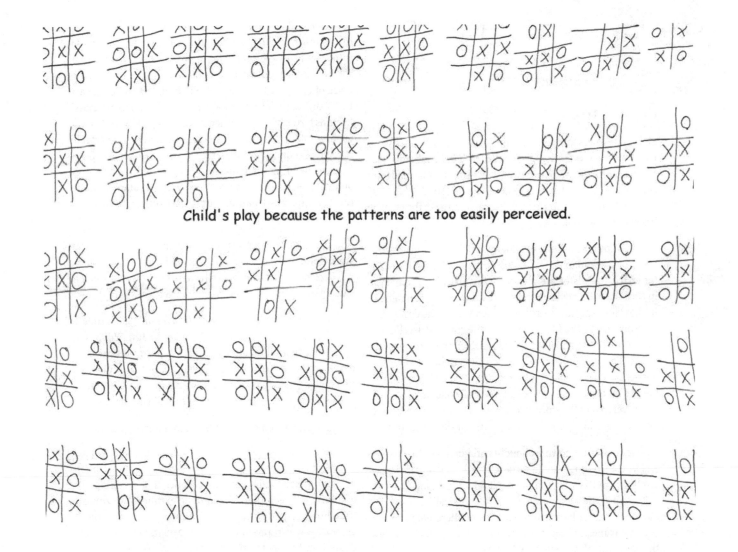

Child's play because the patterns are too easily perceived.

NOTES

Chapter 1:

Cognates: Words that derive from a common root and are similar in meaning even though they are in a different language. Languages frequently borrow words from one another and thus similar words in different languages can be found. Often, the meaning, pronunciation, or spelling can diverge to the point of being unrecognized.

Deaf children in Nicaragua: Many articles have been written on Nicaraguan Sign Language, also called NSL or ISN (after the initials of the phrase in Spanish). Deaf children in Nicaragua did not have access to each other, nor to training in sign language, until 1979, when schools for the deaf began to be opened. Over a few generations, the children developed a fully functional sign language that enabled them to communicate. This is believed to be the first time in history that scientists have been able to observe a language spontaneously created (as opposed to created intentionally like Esperanto). A good overview of the story can be found at www.nytimes.com/library/magazine/home/19991024mag-sign-language.html.

Tic-tac-toe: Also known as noughts and crosses. Tic-tac-toe, and its cousins go-moku (a game where the board is variously 13x13 or 15x15 and you have to get 5 in a row) and *Qubic* (a 4x4x4 cube) are all amenable to mathematical analysis. Tic-tac-toe in particular is fairly trivial since there only 125,168 possible games. If both players employ the optimal strategy, the game will always end in a draw.

NP-hard and NP-complete: These are terms from complexity theory, the field of mathematics that studies how hard it is to solve a given problem (as opposed to whether it can be solved at all, which is called "computability theory"). Other types of complexity include P, NP, PSPACE-complete, and EXPTIME-complete. Many abstract board games are classifiable as terms of their mathematical complexity in this way; for example, checkers is EXPTIME-complete, and *Othello* is PSPACE-complete. Rendering games obsolete is a favorite pastime of mathematicians. They have proven that for optimal players, the first player to move will always win tic-tac-toe and also games such as *Connect Four* and *Pentominoes.*

Sisyphean task: Sisyphus was condemned to roll a heavy stone uphill in Hell. Every time he got it to the top, it would roll back down again and he'd have to do it over. In modern video games, this is called "restoring a save."

Mentally challenging games and Alzheimer's: A study in the *New England Journal of Medicine* in June 2003 indicated that mental challenges such as games retarded the development of Alzheimer's. Games weren't the only mental challenge studied; playing musical instruments, learning new languages, and dancing also had similar effects.

Mu ha ha ha: A common gloat heard in Internet gaming.

Games as vertices: Many games that require you to place one piece adjacent to another can be expressed as problems in graph theory, a field of mathematics that studies points and links between them. Each node is called a *vertex,* and each link is called an *edge.* Analyzing games in this highly abstract way can reveal many fundamental characteristics about how to play them well.

Chapter 2:

Game theory: A field of mathematics that studies decision making in formal models. Most games can be interpreted as formal models, but game theory tends to run afoul of real-world data when the mathematical hypotheses are tested, largely because game theory is based on optimal strategies. Most people aren't optimal all the time. Game theory doesn't help you design a better game, but it can help explain why people make certain choices in a game.

Roger Caillois: An anthropologist who wrote a book called *Man, Play and Games* in 1958. In it, he also categorized games into four types based on chance, competition, make-believe or pretense, and vertigo. He saw games primarily as tools of acculturation.

Johan Huizinga: Author of *Homo Ludens* (1938), a book primarily focusing on the importance of play in human culture. Huizinga defines the concept of the "magic circle" within which play takes place as a protected and even sacred space that must not be violated.

Jesper Juul: An academic who is a leader of the relatively recent "ludology" movement. His website is www.jesperjuul.dk/.

Chris Crawford: One of the grand old men of computer game design, his seminal works include *Eastern Front 1941* and *Balance of Power.* Crawford has long advocated games as art and has also been a major proponent of interactive storytelling. His book *The Art of Computer Game Design* is considered a classic.

Sid Meier: One of the most highly regarded computer game designers working today, Meier has been responsible for *Civilization* (the computer version, not the board game version, although there is now a board game version of the computer game), *Pirates!,* and *Gettysburg.*

Andrew Rollings and Ernest Adams on Game Design: This book was published by New Riders in 2003. It is a solid "how-to" book covering a variety of game genres as well as general game design principles. Disclaimer: I helped write the chapter on online games, so I am biased.

Katie Salen and Eric Zimmerman and Rules of Play: Rules of Play is one of the most important recent books on what games are and how they work. It was published by the MIT Press in 2003. The authors are academics at NYU and also game designers in their own right.

Recognizing faces: The part of the brain that recognizes faces is called the *fusiform face area,* and it's actually used for recognizing individuals of a given class (as opposed to the parts of the brain that recognize classes of things). When people get brain damage in this part of the brain, they become unable to recognize the photographs of famous people, even though they can still classify them as women, men, blondes, young, or old. The fusiform face area has to be trained; most people are expert in other people, so they recognize individuals easily and read their emotions easily. Autistics show reduced functioning of the fusiform face area when examined via MRI. Birdwatchers and car experts show activation of the fusiform face area when they are identifying particular birds or cars.

Filling in blanks and not seeing your nose: Some fun experiments to demonstrate blind spots and the brain filling in known data can be found at http://faculty.washington.edu/

chudler/chvision.html. Many popular optical illusions are based on the fact that the brain makes assumptions about what we are seeing.

The brain…: Steven Johnson's book *Mind Wide Open* (Scribner, 2004) is a wonderful excursion into the mysteries of the human mind.

Cognitive theory: The field of cognition breaks down into several different areas. Cognitive psychology, the mainstream tradition of the field, is mostly abstract and doesn't reference biology very much, whereas the relatively new field of cognitive neuroscience attempts to relate information flow to how the brain works. This latter field is relatively new, and it is what most of the commentary in this book references.

Chunking: According to G. A. Miller's influential 1958 paper "The Magical Number Seven, Plus or Minus Two," our short-term memory (which you can think of as our "scratch pad" for doing mental work) can only handle around seven units of information. If you overload your short-term memory, you'll forget some of the items. Each unit of information can be fairly complex, as long as we are capable of reducing it down to a "chunk," or a collected unit of information with a single easy-to-remember label. This has important implications for a number of fields, including linguistics, interface design, and of course, games—it helps explain why adding more numbers to keep track of in a game will very quickly make the game too hard. Only short-term memory has this limitation; the brain itself is capable of far more.

Automatic chunked patterns: Cognitive science uses numerous terms for many of these related concepts, including chunks, routines, categories, and mental models. In this book I used "chunk" because it's already used in different ways by different disciplines, plus it makes sense on a layman's level. Technically, most of the big "chunked patterns" to which I refer are called *schemata*.

Chunks not behaving as we expect them to: When people learn information, the brain always tags it as "correct" and rarely considers the source's credibility. It takes conscious work to determine otherwise. People also tend to automatically group similar things together in the absence of complete data—thus, a person who didn't know much about either might consider a pumpkin and a basketball to be the same type of object. This can lead to unpleasant surprises when you try to make a pie. There is a field called "source monitoring" within the study of memory that works on examining these issues.

The golden section: Also called the golden mean, golden ratio, and divine proportion. This is too large a topic to discuss in an endnote; whole books have been written about it (such as Mario Livio's *The Golden Ratio: The Story of Phi, the World's Most Astonishing Number)*. The golden ratio is the irrational number, approximately 1.618, called *phi* or φ. Ever since the ancient Greeks, art composed using this ratio in the composition has been deemed more beautiful. Some degree of this perception seems to be hardwired into our brain, perhaps because the ratio manifests in a wide range of natural phenomena, including the spiral pattern of seeds and petals around a flower stem, the shape of curling seashells, and certain proportions of the human body.

Even static has patterns: A concept from algorithmic information theory. An algorithm is an elegant way to describe complex information. The algorithm "22 divided by

7" is a lot shorter than writing out 3.1428571. When we look at 3.1428571, it looks like chaos (it might look like π, but it's only an approximation). And yet the algorithm 22/7 expresses this very big, dense piece of information in a concise manner. What *looks* like highly disordered information may actually be highly *ordered* information—we just might not know what the algorithm to describe it is. Three people described algorithmic information theory nearly simultaneously: Andrei Kolmogorov, Raymond Solomonoff, and Gregory Chaitin, all of whom arrived at it independently.

Three chords and the truth: One of the most basic chord progressions in all of music is the progression from tonic to subdominant to dominant and back again, often written as I-IV-V. In most folk music, blues, and classic rock, this pattern repeats over and over again, albeit in different keys. Music theory states that certain chords lead naturally into others because of leading tones within the chord—the V chord "wants to" go to the I chord because the V chord includes a note that is one half-step below the tonic note. Stopping on the V makes the music sound unresolved. This is also an expression of information theory, in that skilled musicians can intuitively guess what sorts of harmonic structures will follow on a given chord based on their experience.

Flat fifth: A major or minor chord will make use of a *perfect fifth,* which is two notes that are exactly seven half-steps apart on the scale (seven black or white keys on the piano). The flat fifth, or *tritone,* is six half-steps and is extremely dissonant, unlike the perfect fifth and perfect fourth. In much classical music, the tritone is not permitted and is called "the devil's interval." It is, however, extremely common in jazz.

Alternating bass: A rhythm whereby the bass alternates steadily between the tonic note of a chord and the perfect fifth above it.

Grok and Robert Heinlein: The definition offered in the book is "*Grok* means to understand so thoroughly that the observer becomes a part of the observed—to merge, blend, intermarry, lose identity in group experience. It means almost everything that we mean by religion, philosophy, and science—and it means as little to us (because we are from Earth) as color means to a blind man." In Martian, however, the word means "to drink."

Brain functioning on three levels: A good book describing this theory is *Hare Brain, Tortoise Mind* by cognitive scientist Guy Claxton, published by Ecco in 2000. He describes how many problems are best solved by the unconscious mind rather than the conscious or "D-mode" brain.

Approximations of reality: The best example of this that I can come up with is "weight." Physics tells us there is no such thing—mass is the correct concept. But in everyday life weight is "good enough." Another example: hot water is composed of highly excited molecules. But even hot water has molecules that are barely moving (and are therefore "cold"). When we speak of the temperature of water, we don't consider the trillions of water molecules with varying levels of excitation—we instead consider the average of all of them and call it "temperature," a convenient fiction that makes sense for us because we're so big and molecules are so small. Ludwig Boltzmann explained the difference between "temperature" and "individual molecule excitation" as the difference between a *macrostate* and a *microstate.* The schemata the brain works with are macrostates—they are algorithmic representations of reality.

Sticking your finger in fire: The typical elapsed time for a reflex reaction such as this is around 250 milliseconds. Doing it consciously requires around 500 milliseconds.

The football player and instinctive reactions: In the book *Sources of Power: How People Make Decisions,* Gary Klein describes how most complex decisions are made based on the first impulse that came to mind and not conscious thought. Eerily, the first impulse is usually *right.* When they are wrong, however, it can be disastrous. The joke about the football player is funny because it rings true—we recognize something about how the brain works in it.

Knowing what to do on the mandolin: This is also an expression of information theory. In 1948 Claude Shannon developed the basics of information theory, proposing the notion that you could regard an information stream as a chain of probability events. Assume a limited set of symbols (like, say, the alphabet). When you get one given symbol in a sequence (like, say, the letter Q), you can reduce the possible symbols that might come next (like, say, to just the letter U) because you know enough about the symbolic system within which Q and U exist. You're not likely to pick K, but you might think of E for *Q.E.D.* or A for *Qatar.* Music happens to be a highly ordered and fairly limited formal system, and so as you develop a "musical vocabulary," you are also developing a sense of the shape of the entire problem domain, even though a few new letters in the alphabet (such as tremolo on the mandolin) might be new to you.

Practice: Alan Turing, better known as the father of modern computing, is also the creator of something called "Turing's Halting Problem." We know that you can get a computer to tackle incredibly difficult problems. However, we do not know how long it will take for the answers to be returned; no predictive method works. This is because of the Church-Turing thesis, which simply states that you can compute anything that has already been computed—problems we haven't computed yet are unknown territory. Only experience tells us the scope of a problem. In short, we only really learn things by experiencing them.

Mental practice: This is called "mental imagery" and it is widely used in sports training. One study by Anne Isaac in 1992 showed that mental imagery helps an athlete improve in a skill. Other studies have found that autonomic nervous system responses are triggered by detailed mental imagery. It's important to note that actual practice is still better than just imagining yourself doing something—the mental images have to be highly detailed and specific to provide a benefit. One of the most famous examples of mental imagery in this century is shown in the film *The Pianist,* where Wladyslaw Szpilman, played by Adrien Brody, "plays" piano while hovering his fingers above the keys so as to avoid detection by the Nazis.

Chapter 3:

Our perception of reality is basically abstractions: An important paper called "What the Frog's Eye Tells the Frog's Brain," by Lettvin, Maturana, McCulloch, and Pitts, described the fact that what the brain "sees" as output from the eyes is not even vaguely close to the literal visual image. A significant amount of processing turns the literal input of light and shadow into something that the brain copes with. In a very real sense, we do not see the world— we see what our brain tells us we see. Solipsism is five blocks down and to the left.

The map is not the territory: This is a condensation of a statement by the father of general semantics, Alfred Korzybski: "A map is not the territory it represents, but if correct, it has a similar structure to the territory, which accounts for its usefulness." This echoes Kant's differentiation between *Das Ding as Sich* (things as they are) and *Das Sing für uns* (things as we know them).

Run permutations on a book: This statement is a bit too forceful. There exist works of literature that are intended in this manner. Examples include the entire genre of hypertext fiction (*Victory Garden* by Stuart Moulthrop is a good starting point). There are also books such as Julio Cortáar's *Rayuela* (translated as *Hopscotch*) that are intended to be read in multiple different orders. And of course, the genre of games known as "interactive fiction" or text adventures can be seen as a computer-assisted form of this type of book.

Deeply nested clauses: This is typically seen as an expression of G. A. Miller's number cited above: 7±2. In assessing a deeply nested sentence, it's important to realize that each word is itself already being "chunked" from a collection of letters.

The limitations of rules: This is a game-specific way of explaining Gödel's Theorem. Kurt Gödel in his 1931 paper "On Formally Undecidable Propositions in *Principia Mathematica* and Related Systems" proved that there are always propositions that lie outside the boundaries of a given formal system. No formal system can know itself fully. The "magic circle" is basically an attempt to protect the integrity of a model, in the same way that Hilbert's view of mathematics attempted to fully define a system.

Endorphins: "Endorphin" is abbreviated from "endogenous morphine." I'm not kidding when I say we're on drugs when we're having fun! Endorphins are an opiate. The "chill down the spine" effect is often explained as the release of endorphins into the spinal fluid. Pleasure is not the only thing that gives us this effect, of course—adrenaline rushes caused by fear provide a similar sensation.

Break out in a smile: There's good evidence that the smile causes us to be happy and not the other way around. For more reading on emotions, I recommend the work of Paul Ekman.

Learning is the drug: "Fun is the emotional response to learning." – Chris Crawford, March 2004.

Sensory overload: The input capacity of the conscious mind is only around 16 bits a second. Sensory overload can be thought of as the difference between the amount of *information* and the amount of *meaning*. You can have a large stack of information—such as a book typed by monkeys—that is very low in meaning. When the amount of information is too high and we fail to extract meaning from it, we say we're in overload.

RBI: "Runs batted in" in baseball. This statistic is tracked per player and is incremented by one each time a run is scored as a result of their turn at bat, no matter who actually scores the run.

CHAPTER 4:

University programs for game designers: To investigate this more, I urge you to look at the website for the International Game Developers Association and its academic outreach page: www.igda.org/academia/.

Pinochle: A game of cards. You play with a slightly different deck than the standard 52-card deck used for poker or bridge. Points are scored based on the number of particular combinations of cards (called "melds") that you hold in your hand, which is similar to poker, but you also bid for "trumps" (naming a suit higher ranking than all other suits), similar to bridge.

1 Corinthians: The citation is 1 Corinthians 13:11. The following is from the King James version of the Bible:

> *When I was a child, I spake as a child, I understood as a child, I thought as a child: but when I became a man, I put away childish things.*

> *For now we see through a glass, darkly; but then face to face: now I know in part; but then shall I know even as also I am known.*

> *And now abideth faith, hope, charity, these three; but the greatest of these is charity.*

Games with informal rule sets: Many theorists have established a spectrum from "game" to "play." Bruno Bettelheim, the child psychologist, defined forms of play as make-believe (solo or cooperative), joint storytelling, community building, and play with toys. He saw games as team-based or individual competitions against other people or against self-imposed marker thresholds. Of course, joint storytelling or social tie-building proceed by concrete if unspoken rules. I'd argue that what we tend to think of as "play" or "informal" games may have *more* rules than the classic definition of game.

Hierarchical and strongly tribal primates: For marvelous insight into the tribal and animalistic nature of human societies, I highly recommend the work of Jared Diamond, particularly *The Third Chimpanzee* and *Guns, Germs, and Steel.*

Examining the space around us: A lot of games can be treated as problems in graph theory—and this is where those guys saying that the game was all vertices were right. These were people who had essentially "leveled up" in how they viewed space—they were practiced enough in territory problems that they were able to abstract any given territory game into a graph and discern patterns that I, stuck in my perception of it, was unable to see.

Games where things fit together physically: My favorites include *Tetris*, *Blokus*, and *Rumis*.

Games where things fit together conceptually: Poker is probably the most obvious example, but many card games work this way, as do many tile-laying games such as *Carcasonne*.

Games of classification or taxonomy: Card games such as *Uno* and *Go Fish!* and even memory games rely on classifying things into sets.

Cartesian coordinate space: This is the classic method developed by RenéDescartes of locating a point in 2-D space on a grid defined by two orthogonal axes. It serves as the basis of much of algebra (as well as most of computer graphics). This tends to be our default assumption for how space is "shaped," but within graph theory many other types of spaces are possible.

Directed graph: A directed graph is one where you have points connected by lines (vertices and edges, if you like) but the lines have *direction*. Think of the classic children's board game *Chutes and Ladders*; the chutes and ladders on the board are directed links between points on the board. It is a game that does not use Cartesian space; the shortest distances between points have nothing to do with the physical distances on the board, but rather with the number of moves it takes to get to a given spot. All of the "track" games such as *Monopoly* are in effect directed graphs.

You didn't learn the lesson (games of chance): Some wags have called gambling "a tax on the math-impaired." Probability is one of those areas where the human mind just seems to have trouble. The classic example is the repeated coin toss—there are only two possibilities, heads or tails. If you throw a coin and it lands on heads seven times in a row, what are the odds that it will land on tails next? The answer is still 50 percent because of how the question is phrased. If you ask, "What are the odds that eight consecutive throws will land on heads?" the answer is very different (1 in 2^8). Playing on this weakness has been a classic tool of marketers and con men.

Blackjack card counting: Card counting is based on rough statistical analysis to determine what the odds are of receiving a card of the right value next. This is possible because the game is played with a finite deck of known configuration. A detailed explanation of card counting methods can be found at www.allaboutblackjack.com/cardcounting.html.

Dominoes: Because a line of dominoes can only fork when a "double" is played (a domino with the same value on both squares), you can count how many times a given value has been played, and how many are likely to be in players' hands, in order to determine whether it will be possible to play a given number in the future. Assuming the other players are playing optimally to remove the highest-value dominoes from their hand, you can determine which particular dominoes they are likely to have in their hands based on what play choices they make.

Girls as status driven: An excellent glimpse into this world can be found in *Queen Bees and Wannabes: Helping Your Daughter Survive Cliques, Gossip, Boyfriends, and Other Realities of Adolescence* by Rosalind Wiseman.

Shooters: A class of video games where you fire projectiles at targets in order to score points. Usually divided into first-person shooters and 2-D shooters.

Fighting games: A specific genre of video game wherein players take control of a martial artist. Typically, these games involve pressing particular button combinations in order to execute a particular kick or blow or to dodge or deflect attacks. These games usually mimic one-on-one battles.

CounterStrike: A team-based first-person shooter where players play one of two teams: terrorists or counterinsurgents. Each team has a slightly different goal, and the game is fought within a time limit. A very high degree of team coordination is required in order to be successful. *CounterStrike* is the most popular online action game in the world.

Chess and queens: Chess most likely originated in India 1400 years ago. The most mobile piece is the queen, which is allowed to move any distance it likes across the board, be it horizontally, diagonally, or vertically. This mobility only arrived in the game in the fifteenth century, and some argue that it arose as a result of the increasing presence of queens as heads of state in European politics.

Diplomacy: A classic board game of interpersonal strategy, *Diplomacy* requires that players make deals with one another and then proceed to double-cross each other, all in the context of a board representing a map of the world.

Role-playing: Generally speaking, role-playing games are ones where the player takes on an alternate identity. Traditional pen-and-paper role-playing is like a special form of collaborative acting, but the computerized versions tend to put a much heavier emphasis on increasing the statistical definition of your character. A game with role-playing elements is typically one where the character you play can become more powerful over time.

Disgust: A quick online quiz where you can test your own disgust levels with various substances is available at www.bbc.co.uk/science/humanbody/mind/surveys/disgust/. This quiz is part of a study developed by Dr. Val Curtis of the London School of Hygiene and Tropical Medicine.

Groups run by outsize personalities: For more on the many vulnerabilities of the human mind to persuasion, I recommend the wonderful book *Influence: The Psychology of Persuasion* by Robert Cialdini.

Inbred dislike of groups not our own: There are many studies in the history of sociology and psychology that demonstrate this, but perhaps the most chilling is the Stanford Prison Experiment.

Jumping puzzles: A challenge often found in games, jumping puzzles are sequences of jumps that must be performed with precise timing. They are often denigrated as a designer's failure of imagination.

Tile-based: A term for computer graphics that are based on drawing discrete squares, or tiles, each with an image on them. Generally, nothing in the game can straddle the boundary between two tiles.

Topology: The branch of geometry that is interested in the properties of shapes that do not change when you "squish" a shape. In theory, if you had a cube that you could squish all you wanted, you could shape it into a spere. However, to change it into a donut, you have to punch a hole in it. The donut, however, can easily become a teapot.

Platform games: Any of a broad class of games where you attempt to traverse a landscape collecting objects or touching every space on the map. Platform games originally featured platforms as their setting, hence the name.

Frogger: A simple space traversal game where you play a frog attempting to reach one of five safe spaces on the other side of a busy road and a river. Both the road and the river present the same obstacle, but clever artwork makes them look like different play experiences.

Donkey Kong: One of the earliest arcade platformers, this game required you to play Mario, a plumber who wanted to rescue his girlfriend, who was abducted by a giant ape. You had to walk up slanted platforms and jump over rolling barrels in order to reach the top.

Kangaroo: Another early arcade platformer. In this game, you played a kangaroo mother trying to rescue her baby joey. Monkeys threw apples at you from the side of the screen as you tried to reach the top.

Miner 2049er: An early platformer available on 8-bit computer systems, this game was actually very similar topologically to *Pac-Man*. You played a miner who had to touch every spot on the map—as you walked over girders, they changed color to indicate that you had been there.

Q*Bert: Another map traversal game, this game took place on a triangular grid of diamonds rather than in a traditional Cartesian space. It also featured a few spots where there were elements of a directed graph—you could jump onto a little disk that floated beside the map and be taken to the top of the triangle. Once again, the objective was to visit every node on the graph without colliding with an enemy.

Lode Runner and Apple Panic: Complex platformers for 8-bit computers where you were asked to collect all of a number of objects on the screen while not being caught by the enemies. Unlike other platformers, however, this one let you actually change the map by dropping a substance that temporarily removed a segment of the floor. Enemies could fall in the floor and be trapped—if the floor was restored before they escaped, they would be removed from play. Often, objects you needed to retrieve would be hidden under deep floors that required you to tunnel down using this ability, thus risking death. The best levels were highly difficult puzzles.

3-D on rails: A term used to refer to games that have a 3-D representation but do not permit you to move freely through the environment.

True 3-D: A term used to refer to games that use both 3-D rendering and a 3-D space in which the player can move.

Secrets: A term for hidden objects scattered throughout a level of a game. Many games offer up the collection of secrets as an additional axis for success in order to reward thorough exploration.

Pick-up: A generic term for a game object that grants new abilities to the player when collected. The classic early examples include the large dots in *Pac-Man* that make the player capable of eating ghosts and the hammer in *Donkey Kong*, which allows the player to destroy barrels.

Jumping times: An article by Ben Cousins in *Develop Magazine* (August 2002) examined this. The author found that hit games with well-received gameplay had level lengths clustering around 1 minute and 10 seconds, characters that jump have elapsed time in the air clustering around 0.7 seconds, and the elapsed time to perform three combat moves in succession clustered around 2 seconds. He suggests that these should be considered constants for good gameplay.

Time attack: A common tactic in many games, particularly platform games, is to ask you to do the same tasks you have done before but within tighter and tighter time limits.

Atari 2600: The first blockbuster success in the console industry, the Atari 2600's heyday was in the late 70s and early 80s.

Laser Blast: Designed by David Crane, this simple shooter from Activision features a flying saucer with a gun that can shoot at any one of five downward angles. On the terrain below are three tanks per screen. Shots are almost instantaneous, so this is a game of lining up the correct angle and firing before the tanks do.

Quantized: Quantizing is the act of taking continuous values in data and forcing it to fit to a pattern; for example, turning a picture with infinite shades of gray into an image with 256 levels of gray, or taking music that isn't quite on the beat and forcing it to fit perfect mathematical rhythm.

Combos: Many games reward players for executing a series of moves correctly. Often they give a bonus for doing so, such as extra damage when attacking.

Shmup: Slang for "shoot 'em up." This term typically refers to a subgenre of shooter games, ones that embrace the limitations of 2-D graphics.

Space Invaders: The original shmup, *Space Invaders* by Taito featured a tank that moved along the bottom edge of the screen, some barriers that protected the tank but eroded as they were fired upon, and an army of aliens marching inexorably down the screen while firing. As you reduced the number of enemies approaching, the speed of their approach grew faster.

Galaxian: An elaboration of *Space Invaders* that featured some of the aliens leaving the formation and dive-bombing the player rather than the formation moving down the screen.

Gyruss: A spin-off from *Galaxian* that distorted the playfield into a circle. The player moved along the outer rim, and enemies emerged in spirals from the center.

Tempest: An arcade game by Atari in which the player moved along the edge of various shapes, all of which effectively distorted the view of the playfield in what was a fairly standard shooter. Some of the playfields were topologically circular, and others were lines.

Galaga: This sequel to *Galaxian* introduced various key concepts such as bonus levels and power-ups (your ship could be captured and then recaptured so that you earned double firepower).

Gorf: A whimsical arcade shooter that featured notably different opponents on different levels, including a mothership as a final enemy for stages.

Zaxxon: Isometric scrolling shooters are not unheard of, but they are usually merely visual tricks to spice up a shooter that is truly a 2-D experience. *Zaxxon,* however, permitted movement along the vertical axis and had obstacles and targets at different heights. The perspective made it tricky to align the ship, but the graphics were amazing for its time. Very few other games made use of this style of gameplay, with the notable exception of *Blue Max* and its sequel, which set the gameplay in World War I and included the ability to bomb targets.

Centipede: One of the most charming shoot-'em-ups ever made, *Centipede* was notable for its extension of several key concepts from earlier games. It permitted full planar movement within a restricted area at the bottom of the screen, allowing enemies to inhabit the space *behind* the player. It made use of the same sort of barriers that *Space Invaders* had, only it characterized them as mushrooms and spread them across the entire screen. It had a wide assortment of enemies, some of which marched down the screen and some of which were dive-bombers. Finally, the control mechanism was a trackball, which gave players control over acceleration rather than just linear movement speed as joystick-controlled shooters did.

Asteroids: A shooter played on a toroidal field. The torus was never displayed to the user as such, of course; they were presented with a stark black screen with asteroids drifting on it. The top and bottom edges wrapped around, as did the left and right edges. Every time you shot an asteroid, it broke into smaller pieces. Only the smaller pieces could be removed from play. You controlled your ship using a reasonable 2-D simulation of inertial physics. Most people chose not to move very much and instead played the game as a turret, as it was difficult to control your ship.

Robotron: One of several classic games developed by Williams during a very fertile period for game innovation there. In *Robotron,* control requires two joysticks, one for movement and another to fire in any of eight directions. The field is a simple rectangle filled with enemy robots and with humans you must try to save. Should a robot contact a human, the human is killed. Collecting the humans gave extra points, but advancing to the next level was based on slaying all the robots.

Defender: Another Williams game featuring rescue, *Defender* made the importance of protecting your humans even more critical. The gameplay field was a long wrapping ribbon, and players were able to move freely all the way around the surface of the ribbon. At the bottom of the ribbon were humans, and from the top descended a variety of aliens. Some sorts of aliens would attack you directly, but others would locate humans and carry them to the top of the screen. Once captured in this way, the humans became extremely dangerous enemies that hunted you down. *Defender* was famous for an extremely difficult control interface as well.

Choplifter: An 8-bit computer game developed by Broderbund. In *Choplifter,* you played a helicopter pilot on a long oblong field that scrolled in both directions. An enemy convoy marched from one end of the field to the other. In its path were buildings full of humans you had to fly out to, rescue, and return to your base at the other end. Although you could spend your time shooting the enemy, your score was based on your success at the humanitarian goal

rather than the destructive one.

Bosses: A generic term for any enemy that is notably larger and more powerful than those that came before, typically placed at the end of a series of thematically linked levels.

Tetris: An abstract puzzle game designed by Alexei Pajitnov. Played on a grid that is taller than it is wide, this game features pieces each composed of four smaller squares falling from the top of the field. The player is allowed to move the pieces from side to side as they fall and to rotate them in place. Should the pieces pile up to the top of the field, the game is over. When a full horizontal row is created, all the squares on that row are deleted and the pieces above fall down to take their place.

Hexagons: The *Tetris* variant with hexagons was, naturally enough, called *Hextris.* However, it did not make use of pieces with six hexagons and therefore didn't have the clever pun in the title of the original *Tetris.*

3-D Tetris: Many variants were created, from Pajitnov's own *Welltris,* which was really four separate games of Tetris played on a cross-shaped field, to true 3-D variants that proved to be extraordinarily difficult to play and never garnered much acceptance.

Chapter 5:

"King me": The phrase spoken when you move a checkers piece to the last row on the board. There's an interesting political undertone to checkers, in that it is assumed that common soldiers must only charge forward, whereas kings have more freedom of movement (and may retreat)—and yet, it is also assumed that any soldier may become a king.

Abstract games: In the gamer community, religious wars occur over whether or not a game should include fictional dressing or not. There is an entire genre of abstract strategy games that is arguably not enhanced by the inclusion of back story or art treatments.

Deathrace: This was also the first instance of a movie being adapted to a game.

Deathrace 2000: Movie released in 1975, starring David Carradine and Sylvester Stallone. It is about cross-country racing in the future; running over pedestrians scores points in the race, and some fans are crazed enough to throw themselves under the wheels of their favorite drivers to help them win.

Effects of media on violence: An ongoing debate among academics. Most of the evidence is limited to demonstrating a rise in aggressive behavior for a few minutes—hardly advanced mind control. Others feel that vicarious exploration of violence is natural and even a necessary part of development. For a representative look at this position, try Gerard Jones's *Killing Monsters: Why Children Need Fantasy, Super Heroes, and Make-Believe Violence,* published by Basic Books in 2003. In addition, the American Academy of Family Physicians determined that there was insufficient evidence to make a link between video games and violence, www.aafp.org/afp/20020401/tips/1.html.

School shootings: Several school shootings have been blamed on the effects of video games. There have also been cases of criminals claiming inspiration from acts of crime in video games. The industry's position is that games are an art form and worthy of protection under the First Amendment and that the responsibility for keeping violent media out of the hands of children rests with parents. In addition, several statistics can be cited to buttress the opinion that video games do not have a significant effect on violent crime; for example, the incidence of violent crime has fallen dramatically just as the popularity of video games has risen. Were there a causal link, one would expect the two to rise in tandem.

Murder simulators: The most outspoken advocate of the point of view that media and video games cause violent behavior is Lt. Col. Dave Grossman, the author of *Stop Teaching Our Kids to Kill: A Call to Action Against TV, Movie and Video Game Violence,* published by Crown Books in 1999. The term "murder simulators" is his.

Cumbia: A Colombian folk dance style in 4/4 with a distinctive "heartbeat" rhythm. It has become popular worldwide and is one of the commonest Latin music rhythms heard.

Marinera: A Peruvian folk dance with a distinctive rat-a-tat beat. It is a highly dramatized courtship dance.

Story written by an actual writer: Two good books on the subject are Lee Sheldon's *Character Development and Storytelling for Games* and David Freeman's *Creating Emotions in Games.*

Planetfall: Designed by Steve Mereztky, *Planetfall* was a very funny text adventure game published by Infocom in 1983.

Marc LeBlanc: A noted designer, LeBlanc is also the co-developer of the MDA framework, a system for assessing games in terms of mechanics, dynamics, and aesthetics. His game design writings can be found at http://algorithmancy.8kindsoffun.com/.

Paul Ekman: A pioneering researcher on facial expressions and emotions. You can read a good introduction to his research in his book *Emotions Revealed*, published by Times Books in 2003.

Nicole Lazzaro: Lazzaro's studies were done by her company XEODesign and were presented at the 2004 Game Developers Conference as well as several other conferences. You can read an overview of the research at www.xeodesign.com/whyweplaygames/.

Runner's high and cognitive puzzles: I'm doing a disservice here to long-distance running, for the sake of the argument. I ran track briefly as a kid, and in fact there are a lot of tough cognitive puzzles to solve when running, such as managing your breathing, the strategy of when to sprint and when to jog, judging stride length and how you plant your feet, and so on. Cognitive puzzles lurk in all sorts of places. My main point, however, stands: putting one foot after another to exhaustion isn't fun.

Schadenfreude, fiero, naches, kvell: I am indebted to Nicole Lazzaro for introducing me to many of these wonderful words.

Sensawunda: A term from science fiction criticism. It means, of course, "sense of wonder."

Flow: A term coined by Mihaly Csikszentmihalyi to describe the frame of mind characterized by intense attention and maximum performance on a task. The sensation of flow appears to be linked to increased release of dopamine, which is a neurotransmitter that apparently increases attention ability in the frontal cortex. Evidence seems to be mounting that dopamine is not, in itself, the chemical that provides positive feedback. For an introduction to the concept, try *Flow: The Psychology of Optimal Experience*, published in 1991 by Perennial.

CHAPTER 6:

Bell curve distribution of IQ: The standard IQ (intelligence quotient) tests are normalized around an average score of 100. The tests need to be renormalized every few years because we're all apparently getting smarter. IQ is not accepted by everyone as a valid measure of all sorts of intelligence. There is a concept called "emotional intelligence" as well, which argues that how well we understand and cope with emotions is at least as important, if not more so.

Howard Gardner: In his book *Frames of Mind*, Gardner defined seven types of intelligence, arguing that IQ tests only measured the first two. More recently, he has argued that there are two more types of intelligence: naturalist intelligence and existentialist intelligence.

Gender differences: Two books that provide differing surveys of the field are *Sex on the Brain: The Biological Differences Between Men and Women* by Deborah Blum and *Brain Sex: The Real Difference Between Men and Women* by Anne Moir and David Jessel. For an amusing demonstration of how gender differences can manifest even in simple quizzes, check out the gender test at http://community.sparknotes.com/gender/. Based on accumulating the statistics of millions of test-takers, the test manages to provide a fairly accurate guess at the test-taker's gender.

Spatial rotation: A study in Norway found that differences in spatial rotation ability across genders manifest even in a society that has worked very hard to have gender equality. You can read the study at www.findarticles.com/p/articles/mi_m2294/is_n11-12_v38/ai_21109782. There are no conclusions yet in the scientific community as to why exactly this is so, though of course various evolutionary reasons have been proposed.

Language proficiency in boys: It is worth pointing out again that it is only on average that boys do worse in language proficiency; biological determinism alone does not doom a given individual. In some studies, boys have been shown to have a greater variable range in various skills than girls; for example, both the higher and lower ends of the IQ range tend to be populated with more males than females. There is also evidence, at least in older kids, that coeducational settings cause kids of both genders to shy away from the subjects that are supposed to be better suited to the opposite gender.

Permanent changes in rotation ability: To quote Skip Rizzo of USC, from the transcript of his presentation at the Annenberg Center's conference "Entertainment in the Interactive Age" in 2001: "On the paper and pencil test [of spatial rotation ability], men did much better than women. But when we replicated the test involving an integrated immersive interactive approach [e.g., with a video game], we found women performed as well as men..the important finding was that we found that when we administered the paper and pencil test afterwards, that men and women's scores were no longer significantly different." This is not a shocking result; it has also been seen among deaf kids, who typically suffer from problems in spatial rotation as well. See www.passig.com/pic/CognitiveIntervention(1).htm.

Simon Baron-Cohen: Baron-Cohen's theory, elucidated in his book *The Essential Difference: Men, Women and the Extreme Male Brain,* is controversial, although it echoes earlier theories about Thinking and Feeling brains. Baron-Cohen is an autism researcher, so he didn't come to this conclusion solely from gender research; boys suffer disproportionately from autism and Asperger's, and his hypothesis is that these are malfunctions of the "extreme sys-

tematizing brain." There are some tests online that you can take to arrive at your "systematizing quotient" and "empathizing quotient." They can be found at www.guardian.co.uk/life/news/page/0,12983,937443,00.html.

Asperger's syndrome: Commonly called "high-functioning autism," this syndrome is characterized by difficulty with social interactions and reading emotions.

Learning styles: Sheri Graner Ray's *Gender Inclusive Game Design* is an excellent book covering learning styles as they apply specifically to game design.

Kiersey Temperament Sorter: A derivation of the Myers-Briggs personality type that uses a slightly different organizing metaphor based on the Hippocratic temperaments.

Myers-Briggs personality type: Based on the theories of Carl Jung, this psychometric tool measures a subject's preference for one side or another of 4 different dichotomies. The results can be read as classifying an individual into one of 16 personality types, but in psychology they are intended to indicate preference for given approaches to problem-solving.

Enneagrams: Another personality classification system, enneagrams have nine different types into which people can fall. Each type has two subsidiary characteristics as well; the enneagram is diagrammed on a circle, so the "wings" or secondary types are therefore the neighbors on the circle. Enneagrams are not based on empirical study or psychological theory so much as they are based on the seven deadly sins and numerology.

Hormone effects on personality: Many hormones have been implicated in personality differences, but there are no clear-cut answers as to why exactly this happens, nor can it be usefully used as a predictor. That said, as testosterone decreases in males over their lives, they tend toward reduced aggression. Men convicted of violent crimes show higher levels of testosterone than noncriminal men or men convicted of nonviolent crimes.

Book purchases: The statistic on the ages of women book purchasers comes from the U.S. Census Bureau. For an impressive statistic regarding book purchases by women, consider that romance novels account for almost half of all paperback sales in America. Ninety-three percent of them sell to women.

Female preferences in games: The most popular game genres among women are puzzle and parlor games. This preference is so marked that despite a low penetration of single-player games into the female market, women playing games online make up 51 percent of the online marketplace. The bulk of this large audience is playing puzzle games.

Hardcore players of different genders: The population of women in online role-playing games varies from 15 percent to 50 percent, depending on the game. In comparison, the female market for traditional single-player games sold in traditional channels is more like 5 percent.

Aging game players: Nick Yee was able to graph the differences in male and female behavior across ages after surveying a few thousand players of massively multiplayer online games. Younger males tended toward the more violent activities in the game, and older males tended to more closely match the behavior of females. The percentage of the respondents who were of a given gender showed markedly different distributions across age; there was a huge spike in younger males, whereas the number of females tended to remain relatively even across ages. Yee's Daedalus Project can be found at www.nickyee.com/daedalus/. We should not equate this to the theory of "dedifferentiation," which asserted that as we age, our cognitive strengths and weaknesses get "smoothed out." In 2003, the APA issued a press release about dedifferentiation stating that longitudinal studies had disproven it.

Girls breaking out of traditional gender roles: Reuters reported in September 2004 on a study performed at Penn State that showed that the games played by kids at age 10 had a significant correlation with their academic performance years later. Girls who played sports at age 10 became more interested in math at age 12 than girls who didn't do sports. Girls who spent time on "girly" activities such as knitting, reading, dancing, and playing with dolls tended to perform better later in subjects such as English.

CHAPTER 7:

Cheating during a soccer match: On the flip side, if the referee fails to see that we are offside, we'll take it and often say, "Them's the breaks." It is technically just as bad a violation of the rules, but since the ref (who is part of the formal construct) is fallible, we accept the violation.

You don't get to change the rules: There does exist a game, called *Nomic,* whose rules you rewrite as you play; it's part of the game. It too has limits; you bump up against the physics of reality if you try to change too much. In *Nomic's* case, the changing rules are themselves part of the pattern—but declaring atoms to be the size of Jupiter, or pulling out a gun and shooting another player, are still off-limits even if you make a rule allowing it. *Nomic* was designed by Peter Suber of the Philosophy Department at Earlham College.

Ludemes: A concept developed by Ben Cousins, a video game designer. An article about the concept appeared in the October 2004 issue of *Develop Magazine*. Ben has renamed the concept "primary elements," but I like "ludemes" better even though the word is already in use in a different context. The idea also has a lot in common with the "choice molecules" described by Eric Zimmerman and Katie Salen in *Rules of Play*.

Games incorporate the following elements: This material on basic elements of games is based on a forthcoming talk of mine at the 2005 Game Developers Conference, entitled "An Atomic Theory of Game Design."

The Mastery Problem: This can be summarized as "the rich get richer." It is an expression of iterative zero-sum games—games in which the winner ends up in a better position than the loser. If a high-level player can reinforce their position by repeatedly defeating easy targets, then eventually their position will become unassailable. This is not in itself a problem—it simply leads to victory. The problem arises when a novice coming to the game cannot possibly succeed.

Opportunity cost: Since games are always sequences of challenges, the fact that you made a bad choice cannot simply be undone. At the very least, the fact that you could have chosen to do something else allows your opponent to make their own choice. In playing games, we only give "take-backs" to young children, and there exist a plethora of rules dictating when moves become irrevocable in board games (for example, you commit to a move in chess when you let go of the piece).

Red Queen's Race: In Lewis Carroll's classic book *Through the Looking Glass,* Alice runs alongside the Red Queen in a landscape that is moving very quickly. So quickly, in fact, that they have to run to stand still. This situation has become known as the Red Queen's Race.

CHAPTER 8:

Emergence: The concept of emergence recurs in fields like chaos theory, artificial life, and cellular automata, which are all mathematical systems in which very simple rules lead to behavior that is realistic or unpredictable. Steven Johnson's book *Emergence* covers this topic fairly thoroughly.

Less able to learn as we age: In general, psychological studies have shown that inductive reasoning and information processing (so-called "fluid intelligence") decrease as we age. However, verbal abilities and other forms of "crystallized intelligence" tend to remain constant.

Choose the same characters to play: The tendency of players to repeatedly choose similar characters in online RPGs is verified in my own research.

Cross-gender role-play: There have been many papers written about cross-gender role-play. Males tend to do it far more often than females do, and given the choice, males will rarely choose a gender-neutral presentation, whereas females are more willing. Cross-gender role-play in online games is not an indicator of gender dysphoria in real life.

Apollonian and Dionysian: Another way to think about the distinction between the two styles is that Apollonian periods are often about the medium *as* a medium and Dionysian periods are about what could be *said* with that medium.

Modernism, with its focus on formal characteristics of a medium, was an Apollonian movement; the Dionysian rebellion immediately after included populist art forms such as science fiction and other genres of pulp fiction; the rise of swing, blues, and jazz; and the flowering of the comic strip.

Historical trajectory of new game genres: Many game genres have exhibited the arc towards greater complexity. Of course, often the genre is reinvented with a populist take on the game style, whereupon the curve is reset. There are many genres of game where the complexity has reached a point where only a very few play the games; among them are war games, simulators, and algorithmic games such as *CoreWars*, which required a high degree of programming knowledge in the first place.

The jargon factor: An increase in jargon is also a clear sign that a medium has reached the level of maturity where it can be taught formally rather than through apprenticeship and where the field has enough self-awareness to have examined itself critically. In film, for example, this developed fairly rapidly as film theory was defined. Unfortunately, games are laggards in this respect.

Twonky: The original story by Henry Kuttner and C. L. Moore was published under the pseudonym of Lewis Padgett and filmed in 1953. In it, a device from the future arrives in the past. Its owners cannot cope with it (even though one is a professor), so they get zapped. Even more apropos is their story "Mimsy Were the Borogoves," in which toys from an alien dimension arrive on Earth. Adults cannot cope with them, but the children can—and eventually, they learn enough to open an interdimensional door and go elsewhere, having transcended humanity. So far, nobody has teleported as a result of playing video games, but we can hope.

CHAPTER 9:

Mod or modding: Many video games are constructed in a way that permits players to create variants on the rules, alter the artwork, or even create whole new games using the game's software. This has led to large "mod communities" of player-contributed games and content. This is similar to "house rules" for board games.

Lord Jim: A novel by Joseph Conrad. It is not a cheery book, and the ending is fatalistic at best and grim at worst.

Guernica: A painting by Pablo Picasso, done to commemorate and protest the bombing of that city during the Spanish Civil War.

Software toy: A common appellation for video games that are not goal oriented.

Every medium is interactive: Whether you prefer Marshall McLuhan's nomenclature of "hot" and "cold" media or more contemporary conceptions of audience participation in the artistic construct is kind of academic because it's a debate about the level of interactivity present in only one box in the chart.

Mondrian: Piet Mondrian was a painter who was particularly noted for his compositions that used only colored squares and oblongs.

Disagree with me on this: The game designer Dave Kennerly feels that "shoehorning the principle of the movie, book, narrative, or other inapplicable medium onto the game perpetuates bad games." In his defense, he is speaking primarily of the construction of formal systems themselves.

Belles lettres: Literally "beautiful letters." The term was once widely used as the rubric for all forms of study of writing.

Impressionism: An artistic movement primarily centered in the visual arts and music, it takes its name from the painting *Impression: A Sunrise.* Impressionism in art is more concerned with depicting the play of light on an object than the object itself.

Posterization: An alteration of color and increase in contrast between color forms, frequently used as a filter in image processing software.

Debussy: Composer (1862–1918) best known for *Prelude to "The Afternoon of a Faun."*

Ravel: An important composer in his own right ("Bolero"), but also a talented orchestrator and arranger. The version everyone knows of *Pictures at an Exhibition* is his orchestration rather than Mussorgsky's original.

Virginia Woolf and Jacob's Room: This novel is about Jacob, a young man dead in World War I. We never meet Jacob over the course of the novel. He is depicted solely in terms of how his absence affects the other people in his life.

Gertrude Stein and The Autobiography of Alice B. Toklas: This subversive autobiography was written by Stein writing *as* Alice B. Toklas, who was Stein's longtime companion and lover.

Minesweeper: Installed by default on almost all Windows computers, this game involves revealing a landscape full of bombs by looking at revealed squares that provide information about the hidden neighbors.

Zeitgeist: Driven in part by the rise of photography and also by discoveries in science, the central concerns here became the foundations of Modernism.

CHAPTER 10:

Consider films: Jon Boorstin's *Making Movies Work* is an excellent primer on the basics of film as a medium.

Notation system for dance: It wasn't until the 1500s that the first very primitive system of notating dance was developed, and it wasn't until 1926 that Laban developed a system that was really what we'd call complete.

Prima ballerina: This calls to mind, of course, the poem "Among School Children," written by William Butler Yeats in 1927:

> O body swayed to music, O brightening glance,

> How can we know the dancer from the dance?

Term comparable to choreography: "Ludography" seems like a good choice, except that it is instead comparable to "bibliography" and means the games you have created. This hasn't stopped designer James Ernest from calling himself a ludographer. If anyone has any ideas better than the awful "gameplayographer," let me know! "Ludeme-ographer"? "Ludemographer"?

Games about shooting with a camera: Among them are *Pokemon Snap* for the Nintendo 64 and *Beyond Good & Evil*, available on various platforms.

Hate crime shooters: Several of these have been made, espousing various causes ranging from the agenda of the Ku Klux Klan to Palestinian nationhood.

The Comics Code: Established in the 1950s following an uproar over the impact that violent comics could have on children. The result was self-censorship imposed by the comics industry; for many years, no comics were published without the Comics Code seal of approval. The artistic gap between the EC Comics of the 50s and Art Spiegelman's *Maus* is not that huge—the time gap that resulted from the imposition of the Comics Code arguably set the medium back by 30 years.

Ezra Pound: A brilliant modernist poet who was also a fascist and not a very nice human being.

Lolita: A classic novel by Vladimir Nabokov about an older man who becomes sexually obsessed with a young girl.

Chapter 11:

Gnothi seauton: This is the motto over the entrance to the temple of Apollo at Delphi.

James Lovelock: An environmentalist who proposed the Gaia hypothesis, which is the notion that our biosphere functions as a single complex organism.

Network theory: A whole branch of science has sprung up around a subset of graph theory that studies networks. For further reading, I suggest *Small Worlds* by Duncan Watts and *Linked* by Albert-Lázló Barabái.

Marketing: Yes, even marketing has given us insights into the way humanity works. In particular, marketing has taught us much about mob behavior, information propagation through groups, and the tactics of persuasion.

Architecture affecting people: The classic book in the field is *A Pattern Language* by Christopher Alexander.

Glimmers of hope: The classic example of a game that provides a subtle moral lesson is *M.U.L.E.,* designed by Dani Bunten Berry. In this game of colonization, players compete on a distant world to be the richest member of the colony via participation in multiple industries and selling goods to one another. However, the game also offers an additional victory condition. The overall success of the colony matters. You could win as an individual and still perish with the colony as a whole. The lesson is a remarkably subtle one on the ecologies of economic markets and the importance of both individuals and society.

Chapter 12:

Dani Bunten Berry: Designer of such classic video games as *M.U.L.E.* and *Seven Cities of Gold.*

Duchamp's Nude Descending a Staircase: Considered one of the first paintings to attempt to show motion abstractly, this painting is an early example of Futurism.

Shakespeare forgotten: Interest in the works of Shakespeare has fluctuated over the centuries. Although he was regarded as a solid entertainer in the seventeenth century, and his works were collected in the eighteenth, it is not until the nineteenth century that we see him enthroned as the greatest writer who ever lived.

Epilogue:

Shootings at Columbine High School: In 1999, two students at Columbine High School in Littleton, Colorado, shot and killed several students and teachers. It was later found that both perpetrators were avid players of violent video games, which led to much blame being placed on the games. This is not the only example of video games being blamed for violence. Several lawsuits have been brought against companies in the industry, accusing them of inciting the violence.

Penderecki's Threnody for the Victims of Hiroshima: Krzysztof Penderecki is one of the most widely respected composers of the twentieth century. This piece in particular is highly abstract yet immensely powerful.

Aaron Copland: An American composer whose middle period of work is noted for its use of American motifs and folk tales.

Welles's staging of Macbeth: Orson Welles, best known for *Citizen Kane,* staged a performance of *Macbeth* in 1936 when he was 20. The cast was all black, the setting was changed from Scotland to the Caribbean, and the witches became voodoo witch doctors.

Grand Theft Auto: An extremely popular video game series in the late 1990s and early 2000s, in which you play a criminal performing criminal acts. The games are justifiably admired for their expansive designs, freedom of action, and wide array of fun activities and are also highly controversial due to the subject matter. One of the more reprehensible moments occurs when the player can pick up a prostitute on a street corner, have sexual contact with her in exchange for money, and then beat her up and take the money back.

Pascal's Wager: Blaise Pascal's famous wager comes from his *Pensées*: "Let us weigh the gain and the loss in wagering that God is... If you gain, you gain all; if you lose, you lose nothing. Wager, then, without hesitation that He is."

Funny-shaped dice: These dice, mostly based on Platonic solids, are used to play *Dungeons & Dragons* and other pen and paper role-playing games.

Kinetoscopes: Invented in 1891 in Edison's laboratory, this precursor to the film camera actually used 35mm film on reels, but it required viewers to look into a peephole to see.

WHAT READERS ARE SAYING ABOUT RAPH KOSTER'S *THEORY OF FUN*:

"This book convincingly answers the question, "**What makes a game fun?** And more than that, it dives into topics such as the ethics of games and how games can take their rightful place alongside other respected forms of entertainment. It's all good stuff, and it's easy to agree with everything Koster writes. It all rings true.

Koster has written one of the best books for our industry. I hope everyone adds it to their bookshelf."

—*Scott Miller, CEO of 3DRealms*

"Raph Koster's *A Theory of Fun for Game Design* is certainly a book worthy of a place on any game designer's shelf. Raph has written a light, frequently humorous, and sometimes touching book that should make a great gift to those of us who have parents or spouses who DON'T understand why we're wasting all of our time with games. Rather than try to explain it to them, you can simply hand them this book."

—*Bruce Woodcock*

"Entertaining, thoughtful, an excellent job."

—*Slashdot*

"Every once in a while a short and simple book comes along that manages to describe a really huge concept that applies to numerous aspects of life. I'm not sure if the author intended to, but when you scrutinize this book I found more applicable thoughts and views than I did while looking through Confucius."

—*Theis Egeberg, Denmark*

"Entertaining and innovative... a wide-ranging intellectual foray into what games mean."

—*BlogCritics.org*

"This book not only is an entertaining read, but also presents a vocabulary of valuable tools for game developers across all media. So many books are written these days on the techniques of designing games. But without understanding *why* we play games, all that technique is meaningless."

—*Scott Tengelin*

"It's a book I sincerely believe **everyone** should have read at least once in their lifetime. It's that important... what Campbell and Vogler did to storytelling, Koster has done to *play*. This is a seriously important work. It's a pop-science book that makes use of the very theory it espouses. And it works. It works exceptionally well. By the time you've read through it, so many pieces of the game design puzzle will have clicked together in your head that you'll sit there wondering how someone could get so much knowledge across in such an easily swallowed pill... This book is history in the making. It will be referred to in seminal books whose authors have not yet even been born."

—*GameDev.net*

"Thankfully, *A Theory of Fun* exceeded my expectations on all levels. It has the accessibility of *Understanding Comics*, having a narrative depicted in images on every other page. But it also has the depth, having the text to go along with it all, unlike *Understanding Comics*. It's thoroughly researched and well written. Best of all it gives good solid insights. You come out knowing more and being able to think about things in new and interesting ways. Although it is all firmly based around games, the book jumps through many disciplines—mathematics, psychology, art, and so forth. When the author touches on complex items, he cuts to the chase about how it's applicable to the subject matter. In summary, I think it's an excellent book and an instant classic."

—*Jonathan, from Bookham, Surrey, UK*

"It is an insightful read from a thoughtful industry insider, and equally notable, it is provocative for the questions it raises."

—*terranova.blogs.com*

"I'm really glad that you wrote this! Everyone from professional game developers to those who want to understand why we play games will enjoy *A Theory of Fun*. You've written a wonderful starting point for research and many future dinner conversations!"

—*Cory Ondrejka, VP, Linden Lab*

"Koster tries to describe why a computer game is enjoyable, or at least what makes the successful ones so. En route, he gives an informal synopsis and taxonomy of the games that have appeared since the 1970s—the seminal Space Invaders, Pac Man, Defender, Tempest, and others from your misspent youth. (Well, mine anyway.) Ambitiously, he tries to put games into a broader context, comparing them to other communications media, like music, books, and movies. He craves intellectual respectability for games, on a par with those activities, for which academic analysis is now commonplace. Koster suggests that with now over 20 years of gaming, it is likewise time for games to be regarded seriously."

—*Dr. Wes Boudville, Java developer*

"I'll never look at game design in quite the same way again."

—*Grimwell.com*

"This entertaining and innovative book is ostensibly for game designers. Personally, I think it is more than that: it's a primer for anyone interested in games, both for how they work and what we think of them. Written by Raph Koster, the chief creative officer for Sony Online Entertainment, it isn't an artificial or inflated study in how to build a particular kind of game. Instead, it is a wide-ranging intellectual foray into what games mean, both to individuals and society, and how they operate on a host of different levels."

—*Wallowworld.com*

"A thoughtful and entertaining book that distills years of experience and research from a great and practical game designer. Koster explores the fun of games from many angles such as personal experience, academic research, anecdotes, and cognitive neuroscience. The core of the book establishes the role of games, why games are fun or boring, the elements of beauty and delight, and the beginnings of a framework for the critical analysis of video games. Along the way, Koster provides a justification for video games as practical teaching tools, a viable and important medium for art, and a legitimate part of our culture.

The writing style makes it approachable to casual readers or game designers. Every other page is a thoughtful cartoon, interwoven with the rich text. This makes it read like two books carefully spliced together—in a good way. As a software professional working in the industry, I especially appreciated the comprehensive end notes."

—*Patrick McCuller*

"You should buy the book immediately."

—*Dr. Richard Bartle*

"This is the only book in a life of 'tube' reading that a stranger has stopped me to ask what I was reading. It is the Gita of gaming."

—*Jason Cason, UK*

"A great book that explores what is necessary and sufficient for a game (particularly video games) to be fun. His premise is that the fun most associated with games is the enjoyment gained from learning how to play the game, and learning how to better play the game. Games are so good at conveying this fun because they are little sandboxes; the player doesn't have to worry about dying, so they'll be able to explore more exciting (and dangerous) worlds than are possible in the real world."

- *David Ganzhorn*

"I've handed out close to 15 copies of this book so far…"

—*Paul Stephanouk, Big Huge Games*